Sanskrit

The Original Source of European Languages

By

Prof. Ravi Prakash Arya

Chair Professor

Maharshi Dayanand Chair (UGC)

Maharshi Dayanand University, Rohtak

Amazon Books, USA

In association with

Indian Foundation for Vedic Science

1051, Sector-1, Rohtak, Haryana, India, Pin -124001

Contact No. 09313033917; 09650183260

Email:vedicscience@rediffmail.com;vedicscience@gmail.com

Second Edition

Kali era: 5123 (c. 2021)
Kalpa era : 1,97,29,49,123
Brahma era: 15,55,21,97,29,49,123

ISBN 9788187710271

Contents

	Page
Sanskrit: The Original Source of English Language	5
Evolution of English Grammatical Structure	44
Origin of English months	51
Evolution of the Lithuanian Language	58
Evolution of the Avesta Language	60
Evolution of the Greek Language	64
Evolution of the Latin Language	66
Evolution of Old Slav. and other Slavic languages	68
Sanskrit Origin of Numbers in the World Languages	76
Chart 1 (Numerals from No. 1 to No. 5)	76
Chart 1 (Numerals from No. 6 to No. 10)	89
References	102

1

Sanskrit

The Original Source of English language

All the languages of the world have an interesting and long history of their origin and development. All of them have stemmed from their original source, Sanskrit (Vedic Sanskrit) just like various off-shoots of a tree. Some of them are directly associated with their origin and so they are easily cognizable and decipherable. Some of them, having passed through labyrinthine process of their development, indirectly and traditionally find their association with the novel inhabitants and having influenced by their new physiological, geographical and sociological backgrounds lost their originality and assumed altogether a new distinct form thus giving rise to a new family or class of languages. Nevertheless, in a way or other they have also evolved from one common source *i.e.*Sanskrit (Vedic Sanskrit). It is true what Maharshi Dayananda Sarasvati once observed "Therefore the Veda was expressed in Sanskrit, which is not the language of any particular region of the globe and the Vedic Language is the root cause of all other languages of the world"[1]

"Sanskrit is the root cause of all the languages"[2]

Most of the European scholars could not help praise the wonderful and copious structure of the Sanskrit language. William Jones pronounced the Sanskrit language to be 'of a wonderful structure, more perfect than the Greek, more copious than the Latin, and more exquisitely refined than either.'(*Asiatic Researches*, Vol. 1, p. 422). Prof. Bopp (*Edinborough Review*,

---

[1]इसलिए संस्कृत में ही वेद का प्रकाश किया जो किसी देश की भाषा नहीं और वेदभाषा अन्य सब भाषाओं का कारण है। See Bharatiya,V.S.2042: 28-29

[2]*SatyārthaPrakāsa, Chapter* 7.

Vol, XXXIII, p. 43) also had to confess that 'Sanskrit is more perfect and copious than the Greek and the Latin and more exquisite and eloquent than either. Prof. Max Mueller (*Science of Language*, p.203) had to declare Sanskrit '*Language of languages*'. He remarked that 'It has been truly said that Sanskrit is to the science of language what Mathematics is to Astronomy.' Prof. Heeren (*Historical Researches*, Vl.XXXIII, p.43) recalls Sanskrit 'to be one of the richest and most refined of any. It has, moreover, reached a high degree of cultivation, and the richness of its philosophy is in no way inferior to its poetic beauties, as it presents us with an abundance of technical terms to express the most abstract ideas.' Inspite of all their praises the western scholars, linguists or philologists were reluctant to accept Sanskrit as the original source of all languages. To hide this fact, they advanced their own surmises and developed a new idea of the existence of Proto-Indo European language which is held as a common source of all Indo-European languages. This idea is merely based on supposition and has no confirmed or valid footing behind it and as such no genuine researcher who has troubled his head a little bit in this direction cannot hold this baseless and false assumption valid. Many scholars have already challenged its validity and disapproved of it. In the words of Lt. Col. Vans Kennedy :

> "Are there any indications in history, tradition, or affinity of language, which evince that a primeval tongue did actually exist 1200 years B.C. from which Greek and Sanskrit were derived? But it is evidently impossible to answer this question in the affirmative, or to produce any proofs of the prevalence of such a primeval tongue."

He goes further on to confirm the originality of Sanskrit as:

> "And the mere prevalence of such a primeval tongue; and the mere supposition, therefore that it may have existed is not sufficient to disapprove the perfect originality of Sanskrit."

He again questions the entity of primeval tongue :

> "If that tongue existed where, then, are the words of this primeval tongue to be found, and, if it be now extinct, how are the words supposed to belong to it and to be still preserved in Sanskrit to be ascertained,"

At last, we can safely and unhesitatingly maintain that

supposition has no place in science and any inference made out of supposed statements can never be the science, but the travesty of science which would lead to the permanent closure of the subject under discussion. So if we want to open up further vistas of research in the field of origin and development of languages, we shall have to drop the idea of the existence of Proto-Indo-European language and shall have to concentrate around Sanskrit which is evidently and undisputedly is the source of all other languages.[1]

The present work is dedicated to the problem of origin and development languages in general and European languages in particular. Every Indian is well aware of the fact that all Indian vernaculars have sprung up from their mother, Sanskrit. English is only the foreign tongue that is widely spoken in India. So it would be interesting and pleasing to every Indian to know how this language was also born or evolved traditionally from Sanskrit. In this regard, we get the first clue from Maharishi Dayananda's statement made by him during the course of his lectures in Pune. On Saturday, July 10,1875, he spoke thus :

> "Sanskrit is the root cause of all the languages. The languages like English found their origin or genesis traditionally in Sanskrit. One Language degenerates from the other. English 'we' sprang up from Sanskrit *vayam*with the vocalization of *vayam.* Similarly from *pitara*(Sanskrit) came pater (Latin) and father (English); from *yuyam*came 'you' and from *ādim,* 'Adem', etc. This type of degeneration is sometimes bound with certain rules and sometimes takes place accidentally. No explanation is needed to scholars in this regard."[2]

---

1 In this regard we may also refer to Dr. Gopal (1983: Intro. 3). According to him, "Although a common Indo-European Origin for all cognate words found in Sanskrit, Greek and Latin is postulated by modern philologists and Sanskrit is not accepted as their primary source, it cannot be gainsaid that the oldest form of cognate words has been preserved in the Vedic language."

2 संस्कृत सारी भाषाओं का मूल है। अंग्रेजी सदृश भाषाएं उससे परम्परा से उपन्न हुई। एक भाषा दूसरी भाषा का अपभ्रंश होकर उत्पन्न होती है। 'वयम' इस शब्द के 'यम' को सम्प्रसारण होकर अंग्रेजी का 'वूई' (we) यह शब्द उत्पन्न हुआ। उसी

Before I explain and elucidate this idea of thetraditional evolution of English, I would like to quote Mary Serjeantson who devoted his lot of precious time to search out foreign loan words in English. Though the author of the present lines does not fully agree with his observations, still some of his findings and conclusions shed an ample good light on how English finds a traditional origin in Sanskrit by inheriting words from it through Greek and Latin? He observes, thus:

> "English has borrowed a few words, some directly and some indirectly, from Sanskrit, and these are among the very latest and very earliest from the East. Already in the old English period, and previously on the continent (as has been pointed out in chapter II), a few Sanskrit words had passed into Germanic or English through Greek and Latin."[1]

Here Mary Serjeantson makes a mention of a few Sanskrit words only, but I have discovered a long list of words which were inherited by English from its mother, Sanskrit either directly or through many other European Languages.

Here is the list of Sanskrit words which are borrowed traditionally by English via many other European languages.

(List showing traditional evolution of Englishvocabulary from Sanskrit.

प्रकार 'पितर' से 'पेतर' (लैटिन) और फादर (अंग्रेजी) 'यूयम' से 'यू' (you) और आदिम से आदम (Adam) इत्यादि। ऐसे अपभ्रंश यथेच्छाचार से भी होतेहैं। इसके बारे में बुद्धिमानों को कहने की कुछ आवश्यकता नहीं।

See Bhartiya, V.S. 2042 : 28-29

[1] *Op. cit.* 220-226.

		1	2	3	4	5
1.	*Sanskrit*	*manu/mānava*	*pitṛ*	*mātṛ*	*bhrātṛ*	*svasṛ*
2.	Latin	-	pater	-	frater	swesor
3.	Greek	-	pater	- phrater	-	
4.	Old Slav.	-	-	- -	-	
5.	Avesta	-	-	- -		-
6.	Lithuanian	-	-	- -		-
7.	Gothic	manna	-	-	swistar	
8.	Old Norse	maer	- mooir	-	systir	
9.	Old Saxon	man	-	modar	swestar	
						swester
10.	Old Frishian	man, mon	-	modar	-	suster, sister,
11.	Old Irish	-	-	māthir	-	-
12.	Velsh	-	-	- brawd	-	
13.	Lettish	-	-	-	-	-
14.	Middle Dutch	-	-	-	-	suster
15.	Modern Dutch	man	-	moeder	-	zuster
16.	Swedish	-	- -	-	-	
17.	Old French	-	-	-	-	
18.	Middle French	-	-	- -	-	
19.	Modern French	-	-	- -		
20.	Old German	man	-	muotar	-	swester
21.	Middle German	-	-	- -	-	
22.	German	mann	vater	mutter	bruderschwester	
23.	Old English	man (n)	faeder	modorbrothor		sweoster
		man (n)			swister	
				swyster		
			suster			
24.	Middle English	-	-	-	-	-
25.	Modern English	Man	father	mother	brother	sister

	6	7	8	9	10	11
1.	*sunu, (suta)*	*duhitṛ*	*vāmā*	*vidhavā*	*purohita*	*puruṣa*
2.		-	-	-	praepositus	persōna 'mask'
3.		thugater	-	-	-	phersu
4.		-	-	-	-	-
5.		duyoar	-	vāduvā	-	-
6.		-	-	-	-	-
7.	sunus	dauhtar	-	widuwo	-	-
8.	sunr, sonr	dottir	-	-	-	-
9.	sunu, synu	dohtar	-	widowa	prçstar	-
10.	sunu	dochter	-	widwe	-	-
11.	suth (sutu)	-	-	-	-	-
12.		-	-	-	-	-
13.		-	-	-	-	-
14.		-	-	weduwe	-	-
15.	zoon	dochter	-	weduwe	-	-
16.	-	-	-	-	-	-
17.	-	-	-	vedue	prevost	persone, persoune
18.	-	-	-	-	-	-
19.	-	-	-	veuve	prevot	-
20.	sunu	tohter	-	wituwa witawa	prçstar	-
21.	-	-	-	witewe witwe	-	-
22.	sohn	tochter	-	witwe	-	-
23.	sunu	dohtor	wifman wife-man wimman	widewe widuwe wuduwe	prçost	- -
24.	-	-	wimman wumman	widewe widwe	prest	persone persoum
25.	son	daughter	woman	widow	priest	person

12.	13.	14.	15.	16.	17.
1. *sabhā* (*samāja*)	*ṛṣi*	*paritaṭṛ*	*spaœ*	*gallaḥ*	*donta*
2. civilis 'pertaining to a citizen'	-	Protectus	specere 'To see'	-	dentem
3. -	-	-	-	Glothis 'mouth of the wind pipe'	-
4. -	-	-	-	-	-
5. -	-	-	-	-	-
6. šeima, šeimyna	-	-	-	-	-
7. haims 'village'	-	-	-	-	-
8. -	-	-	spā'to prophesy'	-	-
9. semīja 'family'	-	-	spāhi 'prudent'	-	-
10. -	-	-	-	-	-
11. -	-	-	-	-	-
12. -	-	-	-	-	-
13. sáime	-	-	-	-	-
14. -	-	-	Spien 'to spy'	-	-
15. -	-	-	-	-	-
16. -	-	-	-	-	
17. -	recercher	protectour	espier	-	-
18. -	-	-	-	-	-
19. civilis	-	-	espier	-	denen
20. -	-	-	Spehōn	-	-
21. -	-	-	sphen	-	-
22. -	-	-	spähen	-	-
23. -	-	-	-	-	-
24. -	-	Protectour	spien espien	-	-
25. civil	researcher	protector	Spy	glotin	dent

	18	19	20	21	22	23
1.	*udras*	*hanus, cibuka*	*nakhas*	*nāsā*	*pāda*	*bhrū*
2.	-	gena	-	nāres	Ped	-
3.	hudros 'water snake' 'hydra'	gnathas	-	-	Pod	ophrus
4.	-	-	-	-	-	-
5.	-	-	-	-	-	-
6.	udra	zandas	nagas	Nósis	pedu	-
7.	-	kinnus	-	-	fotus	-
8.	otr	kinni	nagal	Nasar	fótr	-
9.	uydra	kinni	nagal	nose	fōt, fuot	-
10.	-	kin	Neil	Nose	-	-
11.	-	gin	-	-	-	-
12.	-	-	-	-	-	-
13.	-	-	-	-	-	-
14.	-	-	-	nose, nuese	-	-
15.	otter	kin	nagel	neus	voet	-
16.	-	-	-	-	-	-
17.	-	-	-	-	-	-
18.	-	-	-	-	-	-
19.	-	-	-	-	-	-
20.	ottar	chinni	nayal	nasa	fuog	-
21.	-	-	-	-	-	-
22.	otter	kinn	nagel	nase	Fuss	-
23.	otr, otar ottor	cin (n)	naegel, naegl	nosu	fōt	brú
24.	-	-	-	-	-	-
25.	otter	chin	Nail	nose	Foot	brow (eye)

24.	25.	26.	27.	28.	29.
1. *mukha*	*hasta*	*hṛt,hṛd*	*Plihan*	*mudrā*	*hikkā*
2. mentum	-	-	Sptçn	-	-
3. -	-	-	Splçn	-	-
4. -	-	-	-	-	-
5. -	-	-	Spçrçzan	-	-
6. -	-	-	-	-	-
7. -	handus	hairto	-	Mōps 'courage anger'	hixit
8. munpaz	Hond	hjarta	-	Mōor 'anger, wrath'	-
9. mūth, mund	Hand	herta	-	mōd,'mind, intellect heart'	-
10. mūth	-	herte	-	mōd,'mind intellect, heart	-
11. -	-	-	-	-	-
12. -	-	-	-	-	-
13. -	-	-	-	-	-
14. -	-	-	-	moet	-
15. mond	Hand	hart	-	moed	hik, hikken
16. -	-	-	-	-	-
17. -	-	-	Esplen	-	-
18. -	-	-	-	-	-
19. -	-	-	-	-	hoquet
20. mund	Hant	herza	-	muot	-
21. -	-	-	-	muot	-
22. -	hand	herza	-	mut 'courage'	-
23. mūp	hand	heorte	-	mōd,'mind' heart'	-
24. -	-	-	-	mode,mood	Hiccup
25. mouth	hand	heart	Spleen	mood[1]	Hiccou

[1] According to Earnest Klein (475), the origin of these Teutonic words is uncertain, But here it is obvious that their origin can be traced to Sanskrit *mudrā*.

	30	31	32	33	34	35
1.	*mūḍha*	*koṣṭhab-addhatā*	*manas*	*kafa*	*svid<s veda*	*anya, apara*
2.	-	constīpātiō	mçns		-	-
3.	-	-	ménos	-	-	-
4.	-	-	-	-	-	-
5.	-	-	-	-	-	Anyas
6.	-	-	-	-	-	añtras'fr om *anyatara-Skt.'*
7.	-	-	gamunds, muns	-	-	Annarr
8.	-	-	minni	-	-	Annarr
9.	gi-mçd	-	minnea	-	-	andaar
10.	-	-	mine	-	-	ōther
11.	-	-	-	-	-	-
12.	-	-	-	-	-	-
13.	-	-	-	-	-	-
14.	-	-	minne	cochen	-	-
15.	-	-	-	kuchen 'to cough'	-	Ander
16.	-	-	-	-	-	-
17.	-	-	-	-	-	-
18.	-	-	-	-	-	-
19.	-	-	-	-	-	-
20.	gir-meit 'foolish, crazy'	-	gimunt	-	-	Andar
21.	-	-	-	kūchen 'to breath'	-	-
22.	-	-	minne	kenchen	-	Ander
23.	gemāeddge māeded, pp of gemad	-	gemynd 'memory'	cohhian	swat	ōper
24.	mad, madde	-	mind, mynd minde, munde	cowhen caughen	swet	-
25.	mad	Constipation	mind	Cough	sweat	

36	37	38	39	40	41	42	43
1. *tat*	*atra*	*anta*	*upari*	*Tatra*	*Pare, pūrva*	*nairṛti*	*īśāna*
2. topper	-	-	supra 'from Skt. Sarvopari	-	prae'b efore'	-	-
3. to	-	-	-	Parai	-	"eneroi" 'those' below	?eos
4. -	-	-	-	-	-	-	-
5. -	-	-	-	-	-	-	-
6. -	-	-	-	-	prç	-	-
7. -	her	-	-	Thar	faura	-	-
8. pat (that)	her	-	upp	Thar	-	noror	auster 'from the east'
9. that	her, hir	-	-	-	pri	north	ōstar 'to east'
10.thet	-	-	-	Ther	-	north	-
11. -	-	-	-	-	-	-	-
12. -	-	-	-	-	-	-	-
13. -	-	-	-	-	-	-	-
14. -	-	-	upper	-	-	nort, noort	-
15.dat	hier	einde	op, opper	Daar	-	-	oost oosten
16. -	-	-	-	-	-	-	-
17. -	-	-	-	-	-	-	-
18. -	-	-	-	-	-	-	-
19. -	-	-	-	-	pre	-	-
20. daz	hiar	-	uf	dār	-	nord	ōstar 'to east'
21. -	-	-	-	-	-	nord	-
22. das	hier	ende	auf	Da	-	nord	-
23.Thaet	her	ende	up,upp uppan	thāer thçr	fore	noro	Çast 'in the east'
24. -	-	-	uppon uppen	-	-	nora	East east
25. that	here	end	up, upper	There	pre	north	East

	44	45	46	47	48	49
1.	*vāyavaḥpārśvasapta*		*eka*	*duan*	*trayas (masc.)*	*tri* (fem.) *trīṇi* (neut.)
2.	-	portiō	septem	unus	duo dual	trçs, tria
3.	-	-	hepta	oios	dūo	treis, tria
4.	-	-	-		-	
5.	-	-	-	açva	-	-
6.	-	-	septyni	vienas	du	-
7.	-	-	sibun	ains	twai (m.) twas (fem.) tuan (neut.)	threis,thrija
8.	vestr		sjau	einn	their (m) tuaer (fem) tuan (neut)	thrir, thriar thriu
9.	-	-	sibun	çn	twā, twō twé	-
10.	west	-	sigun, seven	ān, én	twā	thrç, threa,
11.	-		sechtn	-	-	-
12.	- -		-	-	-	-
13.	-		-	-	-	- -
14.	west	-	-	-	-	-
15.	west	-	zeven	een	twei	drie
16.	-		-	-	-	- -
17.	-	porcion	-	-	-	-
18.	-		-	-	-	- -
19.	ouest	portion	-	-	-	-
20.	west 'only in compounds'	-	sibun	ein	zwā, zwō zwei (neut)	drī, drīo, driu
21.	west	-	-	-	-	-
22.	west	-	sieben	eins	zwei	drei
23.	west (adv.) 'to the west'	-	seafon	ān	twā	thrī, thrie
24.	west	-	-	an	-	-
25.	west	portion	seven	one	two	three

	50	51	52	53	54	55	56
1.	*pañcansaṣ, saṭ*		*aṣṭau*	*navan*	*daśan*	*pañcadaśa*	*aṣṭādaśa*
2.	quinque	sex	octō	noven	decem	-	-
3.	pente,	hex	oktō	ennéa	dçka	-	-
	pempe				deseti		
4.	-	-	-	-	deseti		
5.	-	-	asta	-	-	-	-
6.	penki	-	astuoni	-	-	-	-
7.	fimf	saihs	ahtan		niun	taihun	fimftaihun
8.	fimm	sex	atta	niu	tiu	fimtanattajan	
9.	-	sehs	anto	-	tehan	fīfiein	ahtotian
10.	fif	sex	achta	nigun	tian	fīftein	achatine
			achte		tene		
					fīne		
11.	-	sç	ocht	noi,	-	-	-
				noin			
12.	-	-	-	-	-	-	-
13.	-	-	-	-	-	-	-
14.	-	-	-	-	-	-	-
15.	vijf	zes	acht	negen	tien	vijftien	achttien
16.	-	-	-	-	-	-	-
17.	-	-	-	-	-	-	-
18.	-	-	-	-	-	-	-
19.	-	-	-	-	-	-	-
20.	fimf,	schs	-	niun	zehanfimfzehanahtozehan		
	finf						
21.	-	-	-	-	-	-	-
22.	fühf	sechs	acht	neun	zehn	fünfzehnachtzehn	
23.	fif	siex,	ehta,	nigon	ten (e)	fiftçne	ehtatene,
		syx,	eahta,				ahtatene
		seox,	ahta				
		seox,	ahta				
		sex					
24.	-	-	-	-	-	-	-
25.	five six	eight	nine	ten	fifteen eighteen		

	57	58	59	60	61	62	63
1.	*pañcāsat*	*ṣaṣṭiḥ*	*aśītiḥ*	*prathama*	*pratiśat*	*ad*	*kṛ*
2.	-	-	-	primus	percentum	edese	creare
3.	-	-	-	prétas	-	edein	-
4.	-	-	-	-	-	jami	-
5.	-	-	-	-	-	-	-
6.	-	-	-	-	-	edmi	-
7.	fimfigjus	-	-	-	-	itan	-
8.	fimmtigr	-	-	jyrstr	-	eta	-
9.	fiftich	-	-	furist	-	etan	-
10.	fiftich	-	achtich	-	-	eta	-
11.	-	-	-	-	-	ith	-
12.	-	-	-	-	-	-	-
13.	-	-	-	-	-	-	-
14.	-	-	-	-	-	-	-
15.	vijftig	-	-	-	-	eten, aat	
16.	-	-	-	-	-	-	-
17.	-	-	-	-	-	-	-
18.	-	-	-	-	-	-	-
19.	-	-	-	-	-	-	-
20.	fimfzug	-	-	furist	-	ezzan	-
21.	-	-	-	-	-	-	-
22.	fünfzig	sechszig	achtzig	fürst	-	essen	-
23.	fifig	sientig	hunde (a) htatig	fyrst, fyrest	-	eatan açt	-
24.	-	-	ezteti	-	-	creare	
25.	fifty	sixty	eighty	first	percent	eat	create

	64	65	66	67	68	69	70
1.	*gam*	*chad*	*jan*	*bhū* *bhavati*	*santi*	*asti*	*asmi*
2.	-	-	-	-	sunt	est	esem, sum
3.	-	-	-	-	essi	esti	eimi
4.	-	-	-	byti	-	jesti	jesmi
5.	-	-	-	-	-	-	-
6.	-	-	-	buti	-	-	esmi
7.	geen	skdus	-	-	sind	ist	im
8.	-	-	-	-	-	es	em
9.	gān	scato	-	bium, biom	sind, sin	ist	em, bço 'akin to Skt. *bhavāmi*'
10.	gan, gçn	-	-	bim	send	is	-
11.	-	-	-	buith	it	is	am
12.	-	-	-	-	-	-	-
13.	-	-	-	-	-	-	-
14.	-	-	-	-	-	-	-
15.	gaan	schauw	-	ben	-	is	-
16.	-	-	-	-	-	-	-
17.	-	-	-	-	-	-	-
18.	-	-	-	-	-	-	-
19.	-	-	generate	-	-	-	-
20.	gān, 'present' gām	scato	-	bim	sint	ist	-
21.	-	-	-	-	-	-	-
22.	gehen	schatten	-	-	-	ist	bin
23.	gān, gā	sceadu	-	-	sind,	is	eam, am
24.	-	-	-	-	sindon	-	-
25.	go	shadow	generate	be	are	is	am

	71	72	73	74	75
1.	*milati*	*luk, lokati*	*carvana*	*dānam*	*vi+naśa*
2.	-	-	-	dōnā tiōnnem	evānescere
3.	-	-	-	doron	-
4.	-	-	-	dani 'tribute'	-
5.	-	-	-	-	-
6.	-	-	-	duonis 'gift'	-
7.	-	-	-	-	-
8.	mōeta	-	-	-	-
9.	mōtian	lōkon	-	dar 'gift'	-
10.	mçta	lōkia	-	-	-
11.	-	-	-	-	-
12.	-	-	-	-	-
13.	-	-	-	-	-
14.	-	locken	-	-	-
15.	moeten	-	kauwen[1]-	-	
16.	-	-	-	-	-
17.	-	-	-	-	`e(s) vanir
18.	-	-	-	-	-
19.	-	-	-	dīnātiōnnem	-
20.	-	luogçn	kiuwan[1]	-	-
21.	-	-	kiuwen[1]	-	-
22.	sammeln cp. Skt. *sammelana*		kauen[1]	-	-
23.	mçtan	lōcian	ceōwan	-	-
24.	-	-	chewen	-	-
25.	meat	look	chew	donation	vanish

[1] The change of *c* into *k* owes to Pāṇ. rule *coḥkuḥ* 8.2.30

	76	77	78	79	80
1.	*smera, smayati*	*seva*	*heḍa*	*kruśa* *krośati*	*vam >* *vamati*
2.	-	servire	-	crucem	vomitus
3.	-	-	-	-	khmein 'to vomit'
4.	smijati, smejo	-	-	-	-
5.	-	-	-	-	vam'spit'
6.	-	-	-	-	vemtú, vémti 'to vomit'
7.	-	-	hatan	-	-
8.	-	-	hata, hatr	kross	1.vāeme 'sea sickness' 2. vāma 'nausea'
9.	-	-	haton	kruzi	-
10.	-	-	hatia	-	-
11.	-	-	-	cros	-
12.	-	-	-	-	-
13.	-	-	-	-	-
14.	-	-	-	crūce	-
15.	-	-	haten	-	-
16.	-	-	-	-	-
17.	-	servir	-	-	-
18.	-	-	-	-	vomite, vomit
19.	-	-	croix		-
20.	smierōn	-	hazzon	krūzi	-
21.	-	-	-	kriuze	-
22.	schmieren	-	hassen	kreuz	-
23.	smerian,	-	hatian	cros	smearcian
24.	-	-		crosvomet, vomit	
25.	smile	serve	hate	cross	vomit

	81	82	83	84	85
1.	*vi, vāchi* *vása* *van<vanati*	*sad<sīdati*	*sī, swap*	*sam+gī*	*pra+car*
2.	vemus 'love'	-	-	-	praedicāre 'to cry in public'
3.	-	kszeathai 'to sit'	-	'omth'n 'voice oracle'	- -
4.	-	sittian	slāpan	singan	-
5.	-	-	-	-	-
6.	-	-	-	-	-
7.	-	sitan	-	siggwan	-
8.	āeskja	sitja	-	-	-
9.	- -	-	-		-
10.	-	sitta	slçpa	sianga, siunga	-
11.	-	-	-	-	-
12.	-	-	-	-	-
13.	-	-	-	-	-
14.	wonscen wūnschen wenscen	sitten	slapen	singher	-
15.	wensen	zitten	slapen	zingen	-
16.	onska	sitta	-	sjunga	-
17.	-	-	-	-	preechier
18.	-	-	-	-	-
19.	-	-	-	-	-
20.	wunsken	sizzan	slafan	singen	-
21.	wansch	sitzen	slafen	singen	-
22.	wansch	sitzen	schlafen	singen	-
23.	wȳscan	sittan	slāepan	singan	-
24.	wisshen	sitten	sleper	singen	precher
25.	wish	sit	sleep	sing	preach

	86	87	88	89	90	91
1.	*āp,āpnoti*	*vana+vas*	*ambara*	*stṛ*	*valabhī*	*vāta,vāyu*
2.	obtenīre	-	ambare ambrum	-	-	ventus
3.	-	-	-	-	-	-
4.	-	-	-	-	-	vejati
5.	-	-	-	-	-	-
6.	-	-	-	-	-	vejas
7.	-	-	-	stairnō	-	winds
8.	-	-	-	stajarna	-	vindr
9.	-	-	-	sterro	-	wind
10.	-	-	-	stera	-	wind
11.	-	-	-	-	-	feth
12.	-	-	-	-	-	-
13.	-	-	-	-	-	-
14.	-	-	-	stjerna	-	-
15.	-	-	-	ster	-	wind
16.	-	-	-	sttjerna	-	-
17.	-	baniss	ambre	-	-	-
18.	ōbtenir	-	-	-	-	-
19.	obtenir	bannir 'to banish'	-	-	-	-
20.	-	-	-	sterro	balcho 'beam'	wint
21.	-	-	-	sterre	balke	-
22.	-	verbannen	Ambra	-	-	wind
23.	-	-	-	steorra	-	-
24.	obteinen	banishen	aumber	sterre	-	wind
25.	obtain	banishment	amber	star	balcony	wind

	92	93	94	95	96	97
1.	*vāri*	*rásmi*	*ghāsa*	*candana*	*jaṅgala*	*karpūra*
2.	-	-	-	-	-	camphora
3.	-	-	-	-	-	kaphourd
4.	-	-	-	-	-	-
5.	-	-	-	-	-	-
6.	-	-	-	-	-	-
7.	wato	-	gras	-	-	-
8.	vatn	-	gras	-	-	-
9.	watar-	gras	-	-	-	
10.	weter	-	gres,gers-		-	-
11.	-	-	-	-	-	-
12.	-	-	-	-	-	-
13.	-	-	-	-	-	-
14.	-	-	-	-	-	-
15.	water	-	gras	-	-	-
16.	-	-	-	-	-	-
17.	-	rai	-	sandal	-	camphore
18.	-	-	-	sandre, sandale, santal	-	comphre
19.	-	rai, rais 'spoke of what'	-	-	jungle	-
20.	wazzar	-	gras	-	-	-
21.	-	-	-	-	-	-
22.	wasser	-	gras	sandanon, santalon	dschungel-	
23.	waeter	rai,	graes, gaess	- -	-	-
24.	-	-	-	sandalum	-	-
25.	water	ray	grass	sandal	jungle	camphor

	98 99	100	101	102		103	104
1.	*horā muhūrta*	*skandha*	*syona*	*divā*		*nakta*	*śati*
2.	hōra 'hour'	minūta	secunda	dies		noct,nox	centuria
3.	orā 'any time'	-	-	-	-	nux, nukt	-
4.	-	-	sunna	-	-	nosti	-
5.	-	-	-	-	-	-	-
6.	-	-	-	-	-	-	-
7.	-	-	sunno	-	-	nahts	-
8.	-	-	sunna	-	-	nátt, nótt	-
9.	-	-	-	-	-	naht	-
10.	-	-	sunne	-		nacht	-
11.	-	-	-	-	-	-	-
12.	-	-	-	-	-	-	-
13.	-	-	-	-	-	-	-
14.	-	-	-	-	-	nacht	-
15.	-	-	zon	-	day	nacht	-
16.	-	-	-	-	-	-	-
17.	ure, ore hore	-	-	-	-	-	-
18.	-	-	-	-	-	-	-
19.	heure	minute	seconde	-	-	-	-
20	-	-	sunna	-		naht	-
21.	-	-	sonne	-	tag	nacht	-
22.	-	minute	sekunde	-	daey	niht	-
23.	hour	minute	-	-		-	-
24	-	-	-	-	-	-	-
25.	hour	minute	second	sun	day	night	century

	105	106	107	108	109	110
1.	*sāmivatsara*	*hyas*	*madhyāhna*	*kuṭī*	*dvāra, dura*[1]	*aṭṭaḥ*
2.	sçmestris	-	meridiānus	-	fores	-
3.	semestris	-	-	-	thúrā	-
4.	-	-	-	-	dvirī	-
5.	-	-	-	-	dvarém (acc. sg.)	-
6.	-	-	-	-	dúrys	-
7.	-	-	-	-	dour	-
8.	-	-	-	kot	dyrr	-
9.	-	-	-	-	duru	-
10.	-	-	-	-	dur, dore-	
11.	-	-	-	-	-	-
12.	-	-	-	-	-	-
13.	-	-	-	-	-	-
14.	-	-	-	cot,cote-		-
15.	-	-	-	kot	-	-
16.	-	-	-	-	-	-
17.	-	geostram	meridian	-	-	-
18.	-	-	-	-	-	-
19.	-	-	meridien	-	-	attique
20.	-	-	-	-	turi	-
21.	-	-	-	-	tür	-
22.	-	-	-	-	tur	-
23.	-	-	-	cot	dor, duru	-
24.	-	-	-	cot, cote	dore, ture	-
25.	semester	yester	meridian	cot,	door	attic, cottage

[1] Cf. *śatadura* 'hundred doors' *RV.* 1.51.3.

	111	112	113	114	115	116
1.	*aspatāla*	*maśka*	*mūṣa (ka)*	*sarpa*	*hari*	*catuṣpada*
2.	hospitale	musca 'fly'	mūs	serpçns	ros, ors	-
3.	-	-	mūs	ksrpein	-	-
4.	-	-	myši	-	-	-
5.	-	-	-	-	-	-
6.	-	-	-	-	-	-
7.	-	-	-	-	-	-
8.	-	-	mūs	-	hross	-
9.	-	-	mūs	-	hros	-
10.	-	-	mūs	-	hors, hars	-
11.	-	-	-	-	-	-
12.	-	-	-	-	-	-
13.	-	-	-	-	-	-
14.	-	-	-	-	ors	-
15.	-	-	muis	-	ros	-
16.	-	-	-	-	-	-
17.	-	-	-	serpent	-	-
18.	-	-	-	-	-	-
19.	-	-	-	serpent	-	-
20.	hospital	-	mūs	-	hros, ros	-
21.	-	-	-	-	-	-
22.	-	-	maus	-	roβ (jumping animal)	-
23.	-	-	mus	-	hors	-
24.	-	-	-	serpent	hors	-
25.	hospital	mosquito	mouse	serpant	horse	quadruped

	117	118	119	120	121	122	123	
1.	*faṇa*	*piṭhara*	*rajjū*	*patra*	*vastrī*	*kapālaswiṣṭa*		
2.	vangenpottus	-	papȳrus	vastiāriumcappe		-		
3.	-	-	-	papūras	-		edus	
4.	-	-	-	-	-	-	-	
5.	-	-	-	-	-	-	-	
6.	-	-	-	-	-	-	-	
7.	fāhan-	raip	-	-	-	-		
			'shoe lace'					
8.	fanga, fā	-	reip	-		-	saétr	
9.	fāhan-	-	-		-	swōti		
10.	fangia	-	-	-	-	-	-	
11.	-	-	-	-	-	-	-	
12.	-	-	-	-	-	-	-	
13.	-	-	-	-	-	-	-	
14.	vangen	pot	reep	-	-	-	-	
15.	vangen	pot	reep	-	-	-	-	
16.	-	-	-	-	-	-	-	
17.	-	-	-	papier	-	-	-	
18.	-	-	-	-	vesliairie-		-	
					vastiaire			
19.	-	pot	-	-		-	-	-
20.	fāhan	-	reif	-	-	swuozi		
			'ring hoop'			chuphsuozi		
21.	vāhen	-	reif	papir	-	kopfsüege		
22.	fangen	-	reif	papir	-	kopfsiüβ		
23.	fōn	pott	rāp	-	-	cuppeswéte		
24.	fangen	pottrop,	rope		vestrye	cuppeswete,	swote	

25. fang	pot	rope	paper	vestry	cup	sweet
124	125	126	127		128	
1. *vastra*	*vāhana*	*manyā* *'collar'*	*miti*		*mātrika*	
2. vestitūra	-		metrum		metricus	
3. -	-		metron		metrist	
4. -	-		-		-	
5. -	-		-		-	
6. -	-		-		-	
7. -	-		-		-	
8. -	-	mon	-		-	
9. -	-	-	-		-	
10. -	-	mana	-		-	
11. -	-	-	-		-	
12. -	-	-	-		-	
13. -	-	-	-		-	
14. -	-	mane	-		-	
15. -	-	-	-		-	
16. -	-	-	-		-	
17. -	-	-	metre		-	
18. vesteure, vesture	wagen	-	-		-	
19. vesture	-	-	-		metrique	
20. -	-	-	-		-	
21. -	-	-	meter		-	
22. -	-	mähna	-		metrix	
23. -	-	manu	-		-	
24. vesteure	-	-	-		-	vesture
25. vesture	wagen	mane	metre		metric	

	129	130	131	132	133
1.	*guru*	*gola*	*kṣudra*	*ulūka*	*kramela*
2.	gravis	globus	-	ulula	camçlus
3.	baros	-	-	-	khámçlos
4.	-	-	-	-	
5.	gouru	-	-	-	
6.	-	-	-	-	
7.	kaurus	-	-	-	
8.	-	-	-	ugla	
9.	-	-	-	-	
10.	-	-	-	-	
11.	-	-	-	-	
12.	-	-	-	-	
13.	-	-	-	-	
14.	-	-	-	ūle	
15.	-	-	-	uil	
16.	-	-	-	-	
17.	-	-	-	-	chamel
18.	-	-	-	-	-
19.	-	globus	-	-	chamean
20.	-	-	scury	ūwile	-
21.	-	-	-	iule	
22.	grab	-	-	eule	kamel
23.	-	-	sceort	ūle	camel
24.	-	-	-	-	chamail, cameil camel, chamel
25.	grave	glob	short	owl	camel

	134	135	136	137	138	139
1.	*kokila*	*akṣa*	*kaksa*	*pavitra*	*romāñca*	*sastra*
2.	cuculis	arcia	classis	puru	-	scientia
3.	kokkux	aninç	-	-	-	-
4.	-		-	-		-
5.	-		-	-	-	-
6.	-		-	-	-	-
7.	-		-	-	-	-
8.	-		-	-	-	-
9.	-		-	-	-	-
10.	-		-	-	-	-
11.	-		-	-	-	-
12.	-		-	-	-	-
13.	-		-	-	-	-
14.	-		-	-	-	-
15.	-		-	-	-	-
16.	-		-	-	-	-
17.	cucu	-	-	pur	romanz, romans	science
18.	-		-	-	-	-
19.	coucou	-	classe	-	romance	-
20.	-	acchus	-	-	-	-
21.	-	-	-	-	-	-
22.	kuckuck	ax, axt	-	-	-	-
23.	-	aex	-	-	-	-
24.	-		-	-	romanz, romaunz	-
25.	cuckoo	axe	class	pure	romance	science

	140	141	142	143	144	145
1.	*sabda, svana*	*nava*	*nāman*	*vāta*	*aphenaṁ*	*ṛchate*
2.	sonus	-	nōmen	ventus	opium	rigit
3.	-	-	-	-	opion	(o) regetai
4.	-	novū	-	vejati	-	-
5.	-	nava	-	-	-	-
6.	-	-	-	vajar	-	-
7.	svanr	nivijis	-	winds	-	-
8.	-	nȳr	-	vindr	-	-
9.	-	nivi, nivuri	-	wind	-	-
10.	-	nīe	-	wind	-	-
11.	-	-	-	-	-	-
12.	-	-	-	-	-	-
13.	-	-	-	-	-	-
14.	-	nūwe, nie nieuwe	-	-	-	-
15.	-	nievw	-	wind	-	-
16.	-	-	-	-	-	-
17.	son	-	non, nom	-	-	-
18.	-	-	-	-	-	-
19.	son	-	nom	-	-	-
20.	-	nivwi	-	wint	-	-
21.	-	nivwé	-	-	-	-
22.	geswin	neu nīwe	-	wind	opium	recket
23.	-	nçowe	-	wind	-	reacheth
24.	soun	newe new	nowne	-	-	-
25.	sound	new	noun	wind	opium	reach

	146	147	148	149	150	151
1.	*kalamam*	*jānu*	*tārā, stṛ*	*kalaśam*	*kupām*	*gala*
2.	calamum	genu	sidera, astrum	calathum, calycem	cupam	gula
3.	khalamon	gonu	teirea,astçr	khvlikha khalathov	-	-
4.	-	-	-	-	-	-
5.	-	-	-	-	-	-
6.	-	-	-	-	-	-
7.	-	-	-	-	-	-
8.	-	-	-	-	-	-
9.	-	-	-	-	-	-
10.	-	-	-	-	-	-
11.	-	-	-	-	-	-
12.	-	-	-	-	-	-
13.	-	-	-	-	-	-
14.	-	-	-	-	-	-
15.	-	-	-	-	-	-
16.	-	-	-	-	-	
17.	-	-	-	-	-	-
18.	-	-	-	-	-	-
19.	-	-	-	-	-	-
20.	-	-	-	-	-	-
21.	-	-	-	-	-	-
22.	kiel	knie	stern	kelch	kufe	kehle
23.	-	-	-	-	-	-
24.	-	-	-	-	-	-
25.	quill	knee	star	chalice	coop	gullet

	152	153	154	155	156	157
1.	*grasate*	*gharmmam*	*corayati*	*cuṣayati*	*sthagatetanum*	
2.	-	thermon	urit	sugit	tegit	tenuem
3.	grasetai	-	-	-	stegetai	-
4.	-	-	-	-	-	-
5.	-	-	-	-	-	-
6.	-	-	-	-	-	-
7.	-	-	-	-	-	-
8.	-	-	-	-	-	-
9.	-	-	-	-	-	-
10.	-	-	-	-	-	-
11.	-	-	-	-	-	-
12.	-	-	-	-	-	-
13.	-	-	-	-	-	-
14.	-	-	-	-	-	-
15.	-	-	-	-	-	-
16.	-	-	-	-	-	-
17.	-	-	-	-	-	
18.	-	-	-	-	-	-
19.	-	-	-	-	-	-
20.	-	-	-	-	-	-
21.	-	-	-	-	-	-
22.	-	-	-	saugen	decken	dünne
23.	-	-	-	-	-	
24.	grazeth (A.S.)	-	churreth (A.S.)	sucketh (A.S.)	Theciath (A.S.)	-
25.	graze	thermal	-	suck	-	thin

	158	159	160	161	162	163
1.	*dame*[1]	*pārāvata*	*na,no, naiva*	*dāru druma, taru*	*pāthaḥ*[2]	*ṛta*
2.	-	-	ne	-	-	rçctus
3.	-	-	-	drūs	-	-
4.	-	-	ne	-	-	-
5.	-	-	ne	dāuru	-	-
6.	-	-	ne	-	-	
7.	-	-	ne	triu	-	raihtsr
8.	-	-	no	trç	bad	rçttr
9.	-	-	ne	trio, tree	bath	reht
10.	-	-	ne	trç	-	-
11.	-	-	-	-	-	-
12.	-	-	-	-	-	-
13.	-	-	-	-	-	-
14.	-	-	-	-	bat	-
15.	dame	-	-	-	bad	-
16.	dam	-	-	-	-	-
17.	-	-	-	-	-	-
18.	-	-	-	-	-	-
19.	-	parapetto	-	-	-	-
20.	-	-	ne	-	bad	reht
21.	-	-	-	-	bat	reht
22.	dame	-	-	-	bad	recht
23.	-	-	nā, nō	trçow	baed	riht
24.	-	-	na, no	tre, tree	bath	right,riht

---

1 *Damehas been enumerated in gṛhanāma(Nir. 3.4) gṛham* doesn't mean 'house' only, but it is also to mean 'house wife'. In this regard, we may note a popular maxim '*nagṛhamgṛhamityāhurgṛhiṇigṛhamucyate.*'

2 In the *RV.* 1.47.33, Sāyaṇa translates *pāthas* as 'taken bath.' Actually the same Vedic *pātha* led to the origin of 'bath', etc. in the other European languages.

25. dame	parapet	no not	tree	bath	right

The above-cited examples will suffice to understand the traditional evolution of English from Sanskrit.

Now, I would like to cut short and furnish another list of words borrowed by English from Sanskrit either via Greek, Latin and German or via German only or sometimes directly from Sanskrit. This list also includes those old English terms which failed to survive by the time of modern English and sometimes Anglo-Saxon words have also been incorporated and as such, they have been marked with A.S. so as to separate them from the rests, *i.e.* from Modern and Old English words.

Sanskrit	Greek	Latin	German	English
164. *tarman*	-	terminus	termin	term
165. *tānam*	tonom	tonum	ton	tone
166. *naddham*	-	nodum	knoten	knot
167. *paru*	pur	-	feuer	fire
168. *pardate*	bdeetai	pedit	-	farteth (fart)
169. *puras*	paros	prae	vor	fore
170. *prānta*	-	frontem	frontal	front
171. *fullam*	phullon	folium	blume	flower
172. *phavate*	phvetai	fuit	-	beeth, beoth (A.S.)
173. *bhrū*	ophrus	-	bravne	brow
174. *madhu*	methu	-	met	mead
175. *manate*	mnaetai	monet	meinen	meaneth
176. *mahatva*	megethos	-	macht	might
177. *me*	me	me	ich	me
178. *mitam*	-	metitum	-	meted
179. *mṛtam*	-	mortuum	-	mortal
180. *yat*	-	id	es	it
181 *yuvan*	-	juvenis	jung	young

	Sanskrit	Greek	Latin	German	English
182.	*roṣa*	orgç	-	rasen	rage
183.	*rohita*	ereuthon	-	rot	red
184	*lapana*	-	labium	lippe	lip
185.	*locayati*	-	lucet	-	lixeth (A.S.)
186	*vakṣate*	aezetai	auget	wachsen	waxeth
187.	*varāhaḥ*	-	verses	-	boar,bare (A.S.)
188.	*vastyayati*	-	vastat	wüstet	wasteth
189.	*vepate*	uphaetai	-	weben	weaveth
190.	*śāla*	skholç	schola	schule	school
191.	*śṛnga*	-	cornu	horn	horn
192.	*santaḥ*	-	sanctus	-	saint
193.	*siwati*	-	suit	-	seweth
194.	*sīdati*	-	cedet	-	cedeth
195.	*svanitam*	-	sonitum	-	sound
196.	*hanum*	genuu	-	kinn	chin
197.	*ásanam*	-	-	essen	food
198.	*nābhi*	-	-	nabe	nave
199.	*bandhayati*	-	-	bindet	bind
200.	*bukka*	-	-	bocke	he-goat
201.	*śubha*	-	-	hübsch	handsome
202.	*akṣi*	-	-	auge	eye
203.	*āyasam*	-	-	eisen	iron
204.	*ukṣā*	-	-	ochse	ox
205.	*ubhayata*	-	-	beide	both
206.	*kusyati*	-	-	küssen	kiss
207.	*gati*	-	-	gehen	go
208.	*ghāsa*	-	-	gras	grass
209.	*calli*	-	-	schale	shell

Sanskrit	Greek	Latin	German	English
210. *cicheda*	-	-	schieden	divided
211. *cinatti*	-	-	schneidet	cuts
212. *tṛṣyati*	-	-	durstig	thirsty
213. *dalati*	-	-	theilen	deal, daelath (A.S.)
214. *divyati*	-	-	tagen	daegiah(A.S.)
215. *drākhitam*	-	-	trocken	dry
216. *dhvanati*	-	-	donnen	dinneth
217. *dhvani*	-	-	don	din
218 *palati*	-	-	fliehen	fleeth
219. *fullati*	-	-	blühen	bloweth
220. *pota*	-	-	boot	boat
221. *fullati*	-	-	blasen	bloweth
222. *badati*	-	-	baden	batheth
223. *bhadra*	-	-	besser	better
224. *bhajati*	-	-	beugen	boweth
225. *manuṣya*	-	-	menschheit	mankind
226. *marcati*	-	-	marschiert	marcheth
227. *marddhati*	-	-	marschiert	marcheth
228. *muda*	-	-	mut	mood
229. *laṣati*	-	-	lüstern	lusteth
230. *vardaram*	-	-	wasser	water
231. *vāsa*	-	-	haus	house
232. *vāhanam*	-	-	wagen	wain, wagen
233. *wega*	-	-	wege	way
234. *veṇāti*	-	-	wahnen	weeneth
235. *vela*	-	-	weile	while
236. *stambha*	-	-	stumpf	stupid

	Sanskrit	Greek	Latin	German	English
237.	*sthalam*	-	-	stall	stall
238.	*sthira*	-	-	stier	steer
239.	*syona*	-	-	sonne	sun
240.	*hansa*	-	-	gans	goose
241.	*ajra 'plain'*	ager	agros '*field*'	feld	acre, agriculture
242.	*trikoṇamiti*	trigonov	trignometria	-	trignometry
243.	*takṣaka*	töeikhov	toxicum	-	tonic
244	*ātma, aṇu*	atomas	atomus	atom	atom
245.	*amṛta*	immortal	-	-	immortle
246.	*aveśa*	-	-	-	awise (A.S)
247.	*āvali*	-	-	-	alley
248.	*kuyati*	-	-	-	cooeth
249.	*kurula*	-	-	-	curl
250.	*komala*	-	-	-	comely
251.	*kwelati*	-	-	-	quaileth
252.	*kṣurati*	-	-	-	scoureth
253.	*khalati*	-	-	-	culleth
254.	*khārī*	-	-	-	scar
255.	*khyāti*	-	-	-	quoth
256.	*gaṇa*	-	-	-	ganoth (A.S.)
257.	*gati*	-	-	-	gait
258.	*garddha*	-	-	gier	greed
259.	*ghraṣṭa*	-	-	-	grist
260.	*cāṭa*	-	-	-	cheat
261.	*cūrṇāyati*	-	-	-	churneth
262.	*chalayati*	-	-	-	sylath (A.S.)
263.	*juṣati*	-	-	-	re-joiceth
264.	*jhaṁpati*	-	-	springen	jumpeth

	Sanskrit	Greek	Latin	German	English
265.	*tat*	-	-	das	that
266.	*tasati*	-	-	-	thosseth
267.	*tustam*	-	-	staub	dust
268.	*torati*	-	-	-	teareth, tear
269.	*diyati*	-	-	diät	dieth
270.	*māla*	-	-	männlich	male
271.	*mṛd*	-	-	-	mud
272.	*methati*	-	-	-	mateth
273.	*yāta*	-	-	-	yode
274.	*yuddha*	-	-	-	guthe (A.S.)
275.	*yuyam*	-	-	du	you
276.	*raṇati*	-	-	rennen	runneth
277.	*rudhira*	-	-	-	rodra, icelan
278.	*rodaḥ*	-	-		rodera (A.S.)
279.	*lavan*	-	-	-	leven
280.	*aham*	-	-	ich	I
281.	*mama*	-	-	meins	my
282.	*mām, me*	-	-	-	me
283.	*asmān*	-	-	-	us
284.	*tvam*	-	-	du	thou, you
285.	*tava*	-	-	deins	thine, your
286.	*yasmān*	-	-	-	you
287.	*asau, saḥ*	-	-	er	he
288.	*amūm*	-	-	-	him
289.	*sā*	-	-	sie	she
290.	*te*	-	-	die	they
291.	*tan*	-	-	-	them
292.	*idam*	-	-	-	it

	Sanskrit	Greek	Latin	German	English
293.	*asya*	-	-	-	its
294.	*svaṣādaḥ*	-	-	-	suicide
295.	*purogam*	-	-	programm	programme
296.	*cāru*	-	-	-	charming
297.	*itaraḥ*	-	-	anderer	other
298.	*durbalatā*	-	-	-	debility
299.	*vṛndaḥ*	-	-	band	band
300.	*supara*	-	-	-	supreme
301.	*sūpam*	-	-	suppe	soup
302.	*sīva < siva*	-	-	sähen	sew
303.	*samitiḥ*	-	-	-	committee
304.	*drapsaḥ*	-	-	tropfen	drops
305.	*khaṭvā*	-	-	-	cot
306.	*piṅga*	-	-	pink	pink[1]
307.	*prokṣa*	-	-	-	proxy
308.	*ukṣāṇa* (pl. of *ukṣā*)		-	-	6x
309.	*nakta*	-	-	nacht	night
310.	*gṛbha*	-	-	-	gripp, grab
311.	*baliṣṭha*	-	-	-	bold
312.	*nava*	-	-	-	novel
313.	*balvāna*	-	-	-	valiant
314.	*nava*	-	-	neu	new
315.	*naval*	-	-	-	novel
316.	*naviṣṭha*	-	-	neuste	newest

---

1 According to Dr. Earnest Klein (563), it is of uncertain origin. But its origin can easily be raced to Sanskrit *piṅga.*

317. *preṣṭha*	-	-	priester	priest

Sanskrit	Greek	Latin	German	English
318. *udgama*	-	-	-	outcome
319. *aho*	-	-	-	oh
320. *ullāsa*	-	-	hurra	hurrah
321. *āvarta*	-	-	-	avert
322. *dipsati*	-	-	-	deception
323. *tṛdla*	-	-	-	tread
324. *ava*	-	-	-	obey
325. *vadhu*	-	-	-	bride
326. *śraddhālu*	-	-	-	credulous
327. *śrddhit*	-	-	kredit	credit
328. *daman*	-	-	dominieren	dominate
329. *bhiṣak*	-	-	-	physician
330. *anusvara*	-	-	antwort	answer
331. *svadate*	-	-	schwitzen	sweat
332. *bandhan*	-	-	-	bond, bundle
333. *avāsa*	-	-	-	abyss
334. *svanika*	-	-	-	sonic
335. *vāca*	-	-	-	voice
336. *vācāla*	-	-	-	vocal
337. *antara*	-	-	innen	inter
338. *mādhyam*	-	-	-	medium
339. *pavitratā*	-	-	-	purity
340. *puṇḍa*	-	-	-	pound
341. *lubha*	-	-	liebe	love
342. *lubhāvali*	-	-	liebenswürdig	lovely
343. *vistar*	-	-	-	vast

344. *sīva*	-	-	sähen	sew
Sanskrit	**Greek**	**Latin**	**German**	**English**
345. *sīvati*	-	-	-	seweth
346. *snāyu*	-	-	-	sinew
347. *eka*	-	-	-	equal
348. *dama*	dome	-	haus	home
349. *krūta*	-	-	-	cruel
350. *graddha*	-	-	gier	greed
351. *vid*	-	-	-	wit
352. *jvala*	-	-	-	glow
353. *tapa*	-	-	-	tepid
354. *tṛṣita*	-	-	durstig	thirsty
355. *trasa*	-	-	-	harras,terror
356. *hṛd*	-	-	herz	heart
357. *agni*	-	-	-	ignis, ignite
358. *rakta*	-	-	rot	red
359. *chav*	-	-	kauen	chew
360. *plāyate*	-	-	fliegen	fly
361. *nāma*	-	-	name	name
362. *pāda*	-	-	fuss	foot
363. *krimi*	-	-	kern	germ
364. *ṛju*	-	-	richtig	right
365. *dakṣiṇa*	-	-	dekan	deccan
366. Ātmā			Atem	

Thus hosts of similar other examples may be cited, but the author doesn't think it is necessary to produce all of them here.

2

Evolution of the English-grammatical structure

Besides borrowing a large number of its vocabulary, English owes a lot to Sanskrit for evolving its usage, diction and style. A few illustrations in this regard may be made as under.

1. ***Elision of sounds***: In Sanskrit, the elision of one or two sounds is a common feature. In this regard *Bṛhaddevatā* of Śaunaka (2.116) maintains thus, *varṇasyavarṇayorlopobahunāmvyañjanasya ca. atrāṇīkapirnābhādanoyāmityaghāus ca.*

English has also developed similar tendency of elision of one or more sounds as :

do not →	don't	
cannot	→	can't
will not	→	won't
shall not	→	shan't

2. ***Syntactical placement of 'no'***:English negative particle 'no' had evolved from Sanskrit *na*or *no.* In Sanskrit, especially the Vedic Sanskrit, it anteceds the word it negates, *e.g.*

Nendramdevam-amansata (*RV.* 10.86.1) Yāska has made similar observations in this regard. According to him, *purastādupacārstasyayatpratiṣedhatii.e.na*is placed before the word it negates.

This trend of the Vedic language was traditionally accepted in English. It places 'no' before the negated word, *e.g.* 'I have no book', here 'no' precedes the book. On the other hand, in Classical Sanskrit or Hindi, we don't meet any strict rule regarding the syntactical employment of 'no'. In these languages, it may precede or succeed the word it negates.

3. ***Infinitives*:** Sometimes English seems to adopt Sanskrit forms and rules more perfectly and regularly even than Hindi. For instance, Sanskrit infinitive suffix - *tumun* or - *tum* is accepted in English as 'to'. Sanskrit *saḥgantum (gam+tum) icchati* will be read in English as 'He wants to go'; *saḥ paṭhitum (gam+tum)* will be read as 'He wants to read'. Here, the only difference is that Sanskrit '*-tum*' has changed its position in English from suffix or post-position to pre-position.

4. ***Compounds*:** In Sanskrit Negative Determinative Compound (*Nañ Tatpuruṣa*) enjoins '*a*' before a noun beginning with a vowel (*e.g.an + aśva*). English has also inherited this tendency from Sanskrit with a slight variation. It drops '*a*' altogether and invariably uses *an* as 'un' without any discrimination of vowel or consonant, *e.g.* un-known, un-able, un-do, etc. The other difference is that in Sanskrit *a* or *an* are employed with nominal forms, whereas in English 'un' is employed only with verbal forms.

5. ***Euphonic combinations*:** In Sanskrit, any consonant followed by a nasal sound will be substituted by a nasal or a word pronounced as nasal. Cf. Pāṇ. (8.4.45) *yaro'nunāsike' nunāsikovā.* And *vārt.* (on Pāṇ. 8.4.45) *pratyayebhāṣ āyāṁnityam.*

Examples are : *tad +mātram = tanmātram*

cit + mayam = cinmayam

etad + murārī = etanmurārī

English has borrowed a similar type of tendency. In it, consonants, when coming in proximity with an un-interrupted nasal sound, become silent and pronounced as a nasal itself, *e.g.* mnemonic, mnematics, gnarl, gnash, gnat, gnaw, gnome, gnomon, Gnostic, gnu, knack, knag, knap, knar, knave, knead, knee, knell, knife, knit, knot, knob, know, pneumatic, pneumonia, pneumatics, etc.

6. ***Laws of doubling*:** English doubles its consonants under the following situations.

(i) Words of one syllable having one vowel and ending in a single consonant double the consonant before a suffix beginning with a vowel, such as runner, hitting, knitted.

(ii) Two or three-syllable words ending in a single consonant following a single vowel double the final consonant when the stress falls on the last syllable, *e.g.*beginner, deterred, recurring.

(iii)The final consonant of kidnap, worship, handicap, bias, fuel, the dial is also doubled, as kidnapper, worshipping, handicapped, dialled, and refuelling.

(iv) Words ending in an 'I' following a single vowel usually double the 'I', *e.g.*

quarrel	→	quarrelling
signal	→	signalled
distil	→	distiller
appal	→	appalled
model	→	modelling
repel	→	repellent

English has inherited this characteristic from its mother Sanskrit.

(i) In Sanskrit, a consonant followed by a vowel is doubled. Examples are :

pac	→	*papāca*
jāgṛ	→	*jajāgāra*
bhū	→	*babhūva*
gam	→	*jagām*
dā	→	*dadāti*

Cf. Pāṇ (6.1.1) *ekācodveprathamasya.*

(ii) Sometimes a consonant preceded by a vowel is also doubled.

Examples are :

aṭ	→	*aṭiṭiṣati*
śiṣ	→	*asisiṣati*
riṣ	→	*aririṣati, etc.*

Cf. Paṇ. (6.1.72) *ajāderdvitīyasya.*

(iii) This doubling is also seen with regard to vowels. Examples are :

i	→	*iyāya*
ṛ	→	*āra*

English also exhibits this type of tendency in the following examples. eel, eerie, aardvark, aardwolf, aaron's-beard. *etc.*

7. ***Inflection***: (1) Sanskrit employs *am* affix in the accusative sg. Case, *e.g.*

kim	→	*kam*
asmad	→	*mām*
tad	→	*tam*
Rāma	→	*Rāmam, etc.*

German has also inherited the same characteristics. It adds *am* in the form of 'em', *e.g.*

mein	→	meinem
sein	→	seinem
unser	→	unserem
ihr	→	ihrem
der	→	dem
wer	→	wem

Though English has dropped accusative formations, it preserves 'whom' an accusative form of 'who' where it uses the same affix *am* as 'm'.

(ii) In Sanskrit, nominative plurals are formed with affix *s* or *āsas*(peculiar to Vedic Skt.), as in *Rāma→Rāmas→Rāmāsas.* Similarly English forms its plural with 's' or 'es', *e.g.*

book	→	books
boy	→	boys
army	→	armies

(iii) The termination of genitive singular, dual and plural in Sanskrit are as (*ṅas*), *os* and *ām* respectively. European languages borrowed these terminations as 'es' and 'os' for their possessive (genitive) case. By the time of the modern English, the sounds 'e' and 'o' of 'es' and 'es' were omitted and the omission was indicated by the apostrophe-sign ('). Hence, in English, we have possessive forms like boy's, etc.

8. *Prepositions or prefixes*: Prefixes are always employed in conjunction with verbs. In Vedic Sanskrit, they are employed indifferently after a verb as well as before it. They may be separated from the verb by some intervening word or words. For instance, in *nisasādadhṛtavratovaruṇaḥpastyāsvā̱*(*RV.* 1.25.10), the prefix *ā* is used after the verb *nisasāda.* In *vedā me adhyāsate*(*RV.* 1.25.9), the prefix *adhi* is used before the verb *āsate.* And in *indravāyuimesutāupaprayobhirāgatam*(RV. 1.2.4), the prefix *upa*is separated from the verb *āgatam.*

But Classical Sanskrit attests no such liberty regarding the application of prefixes. It adopts a fixed pattern in their use and always employs them immediately before a verb.[1] On the other hand, German follows Vedic Sanskrit and employs them after and before a verb and also separates them from the verb as the need be, *e.g.*

fahren 'to go'

abfahren 'to leave, to depart'

(i) Ich *fahre* heute abend um 7 uhr*ap.* 'I leave at 7 this evening'

(ii) Sie *ruft* die taxizentrale *an.* 'She calls up the taxi-driver.'

(iii) Herr Fuchs *kommt* um 10 uhr 20 in Frankfurt *an.* 'Mr. Fuchs arrives at 10.20 in Frankfurt.'

---

[1]Cf. Pān. *teprāgdhāto* (1.4.80).

(iv) *Rufen* Sie bitte Herren Beuemann *an.* 'Please call Mr. Baumann up'

But English restricts the use of prefixes (prepositions) only after verbs.

They are used immediately after a verb or sometimes with the intervention by a word or words, *e.g.*

(i) The gun *went off* by itself.

(ii) He *went through* the whole book, but he couldn't discover anything new in it.

(iii) He *called* me *up,* etc.

9. *Degrees of comparison*: In the Sanskrit language, the suffixes -*tara*and -*īyas*form the comparative degree and the suffixes -*tama*and -*iṣṭha* are employed to form the superlative degree.

These suffixes of comparison are retained in the European languages with slight variations. English borrows only -*iṣṭha* for superlative degree and -*tara*for comparative degree via other I.E. languages, *e.g.* Avesta retains the suffix -*iṣṭha* as -*'ista'*, Greek as -'iotas' and Gothic as 'ista'. Modern German retains this suffix as 'ste', *e.g.*

klein	-	kleinste
hoch	-	höchste
teuer	-	teuerste, etc.

English, too, under the influence of German retains -*iṣṭha* as '-est, thus

high	-	highest
noble	-	noblest, etc.

On the other hand, -*tara*is retained in latin as '-tru'; in Gothic as 'thara'; Old High German retains it as 'der'; in Middle German it is retained as '-der' and in Modern German, it reduced to '-er', thus

hoch	-	höher

teuer	-	teurer
klein	-	kleiner, etc.

English, too, following German retains Skt. *-tara*as -'er', *e.g.*

high	-	higher
low	-	lower, etc.[1]

[1] For details see the author (Arya Ravi Prakash, 2007 : Part 1, Chap. 4)

3

Origin of English Months

Romans owe to Indians for the development of their calendar system. According to the author of *India in Greece* (P.142), 'Both among Greeks and Romans - the descendants of colonists from India, continued, especially amongst the latter people down to and throughout the most historical periods.' Thus the Vedic emigrants in Rome totally forget this division of the zodiac into 12 parts. They used to count 10 months in a year and left some days uncounted. They begin with a fresh year with the full moon in the spring season as was in their memory. The names of their months were still driven from their original language, the Sanskrit such as *unus* from Sanskrit *eka*, *duo* from Sanskrit *dvau*, *tria* from Sanskrit *traya*, *quinque* from *pañca*, *sex* from Sanskrit *ṣaṭ*, *septem* from *sapta*, *octo* from *aṣṭau*, *noven* from Sanskrit *navan* and *decem* from Sanskrit *daśam*. The presently extant names of months like September, October, November and December clearly substantiate this fact. According to the Indian *Saurmān*system, *i.e.*the solar measurement of time, the sun passes through the twelve zodiac signs in a year and its passing through each sign makes a month. These 12 zodiac signs were known as 12 *ambers/rāsis*or stars and as result, the names of months were formed after suffixing ambar/amber to the numbers. With the passage of time, the first six months were renamed either after some historical personalities or some specific historical events, though the last four months survived in their original form signalling their very origin to Sanskrit.

The Romanian calendar consisting of 10 months beginning from March as its first month up to December as its last month remained in vogue till 452 BC, when NumaPompilius introduced the custom of inserting 23 days at the interval of two years. But the introduction of 23 days became the bone of contention among the heads of religious sects. This was at last removed by Julius Caesar who with the help of Cleopatra, the empress of Egypt reformed the Romulian calendar after the fashion of the Egyptian calendar. This reform was known as Julian reform or Julian arrangement of the calendar. The history goes like this :

Cleopatra was the empress of Egypt. She was Greek by birth and belonged to the dynasty founded by Tolami, a commander of Alexander. Following the death of Alexander, Tolami declared his domain over Egypt. Cleopatra was from his dynasty. She was born in the 3033 kali era or 68 B.C. Following the death of her father Tolami, the 11th, she took over the reign of Egypt along with her brother Tolami, the 12th. But she was overthrown by her brother in the war of succession. She formed an army in Cypress and tried to recapture power. In the meantime, defeated by Caesar and fled to Egypt a brave soldier named Pompy was guillotined by Tolamy. With the view to please Caesar, he (Tolami) presented his body to Caesar, but Caesar got annoyed at this. Meanwhile, to make a good use of the event, Cleopatra hiding in the precious carpets purchased by Romans met Caesar and he was also taken in by her exquisite beauty. He captured the regime from Tolami and handed it over to Cleopatra. Afterwards, both Caesar and Cleopatra roamed about the banks of the river Nile for many weeks. Cleopatra gave birth to a child who was named as Caesarian, i.e. Junior Caesar. When the queen of Egypt started domiciliating the palace of Rome as a queen-dowager, the artisans, economists and astrologers were sent for from Alexandria, the capital of Egypt. The Roman taxation system was reformed and a new currency was introduced. Roman calendar was also amended by dividing the whole year into 365 days and by adding two more months to the already existing 10 months, after the fashion of the Egyptian calendar. Since the time of Julius Caesar (46 B.C.), the Roman used to have 12 months with the new year commencing with March as the first *amber* (month).

March continued to be the beginning or the legal year in England until the 18th century. In France, it was reckoned as the first month of the year until 1564, when by an edict of Charles IX, January was decreed to be the first month, so that the year may end with December, the months of Jesus Christ's birth.

Scotland followed the example of France.[1]

The history goes further and we are told that during this arrangement, the quintiles amber (fifth month of Romulian calendar and the seventh month of Julian arrangement) was named July by the Egyptian astronomers to felicitate Julius Caesar, as he was born on the 12th of this month. This month was also assigned the highest 31 days since Caesar was the most powerful king of Rome. On the other hand, Caesar also, in turn, felicitated Cleopatra by constructing a temple of the goddess of Venus. Illuckily, Caesar died after two years in 44 B.C. and Cleopatra had to return to her kingdom, Egypt.

Later Julius Augustus also named the sixth amber (sixtilis) after his name as August and also assigned 31 days to his month, since he considered himself no less brave than Julius Caesar.

Similarly, the first amber was named as Mars or March after the god of war. Actually, this was not only the beginning of the year but was the open spring season for waging war. That was why, it was named after Mars, the god of war. Mars being the powerful god was also assigned 31 days.

The second *amber,* April, was named after Latin aperire 'to open' in allusion to its being the season when trees and flowers begin to 'open' and is supported by comparison with the modern Greek word 'opening' for spring. It was given the fourth place in the Julian calendar.

The third *amber* was named Maius by Romulus in respect to the senators and nobles of his city, who were called Majores. Being associated with Majores, it was also given 31 days. It became the fifth in the Julian calendar, which later came to be known as May.

The fourth *amber* was called Junius in honour of the youths of Rome (i.e.Juniares) who served Romulus in war. Since it

---

[1]See*Encyclopaedia Britannica,* Vol. 14. P. 866.

represented minors, it was assigned 30 days. Juniuslater came to be known as June.

September, October, November and December have come down to us in their actual form.

Januarius (January) and Februarius (February) were added at the end as 11th and 12th *amber* of the series by Numa Pompilius. Though in Julian arrangement their place was changed otherwise and they were considered to be the first and second months of the year, but in practical sense, they still continue to be the last months. Since all the additions and subtractions are made to the last member of the series, Feb., being the last one, always adds a day in case of a leap year. These last two months were called January and February, because they wanted the year to end with December to facilitate the birth of Jesus Christ as before. As such the year was started with the newly added last two months only. January, in fact, originated from the Roman term *Janus* which is the corrupt form of Ganesh of Sanskrit. Ganesh symbolises the beginning of every act in Indian tradition, so following the same Indian tradition, Romans started their year with January formed from *Janus.* The next month was coined as Februarius which is the corrupt form of *pravara* of Sanskrit. *Pravara* also symbolises the first of sages born on the earth. On the same pattern, the term Februarius represented the lord of sages.

From the foregoing discussion, it can unhesitatingly be inferred that all the English months can be traced back to Sanskrit via Greek, Roman and Egyptian ones.

Conclusion

On the basis of the foregoing discussion, it can be inferred that the origin of English can be traced back to Sanskrit traditionally via other European languages. Actually, all of the European languages find their prototypes directly or indirectly in Sanskrit.

The close affinity of European languages with Sanskrit will also help theorise the idea that the Vedic language-speaking people must have emigrated from India to colonise alien lands and in course they must have shaped or modified the idiom of the dialects of alien inhabitants.

As regards the origin of the other languages of the globe, it can be maintained that if a consistent thorough integrated research is carried out, all of them can also be traced back to Sanskrit traditionally via other cognate languages.

Thus, Sanskrit was the link language of the world over before long and still, it has the capacity to link the whole world with one stirring of language and these days with the emergence of a new era of computer science, Sanskrit is proving to be the fittest, suitable and scientific language for computer purposes. Hence, the utility of Sanskrit is beyond doubt and now Sanskrit is the demand of time as well as clime.

Appendix- 1

English Vs. Tuḷu Vs. Sanskrit

By the end of 1987, the present author accomplished the task of establishing cognate words between Sanskrit and English and deduced the results that English originated from Sanskrit traditionally via other European languages. But with the beginning of 1988, he all of a sudden, came across startling news heading 'English Traced to Origins of Speech' in one of the leading English dailies 'The Hindustan Times'. According to the paper, an Indian scholar Mr. P.S. Rai submitted a thesis on 'The Primary Evolution of human speech and a million-year-old English' to the Chairman, Department of linguistics, State University of New York, Dr. Mark Aronoff in October 1987. The paper reported that Mr. Rai established over 700 cognate words in Tuḷu and English vocabularies in the said thesis. According to him, modern literary English can be traced back via Tuḷu, the language of the inhabitants of India's south-west coast with which it has striking similarities, to the very origins of human speech about a million years or so ago.

The above news was really alarming to me, as it appeared to have rendered my whole labour worthless. I then managed to acquire a Tuḷu-English Dictionary edited by Professor M. Mariappa Bhat and published by the University of Madras. I went through the whole dictionary to locate the so-called 700 cognate words reported to have been established by Mr. Rai, but it was all in vain. On the contrary, I could locate a large number of cognate words between Sanskrit and Tuḷu. Thus, led by the notion of doubtful authenticity of Mr. Rai's work, I wrote on 9.2.89 to Dr.

Mark Aronoff, the chairman Dept. of Linguistics, State University of New York, referring to the report of the said English daily and requested him to arrange me a photo-copy of the said thesis. On June 12, 1989, Dr. Aronoff replied to my query. I quote hereunder the exact version of his letter.

Dear Dr. Arya,

I am sorry to have delayed so long in responding to your letter. In any case. I have no positive news. Despite what you may have read, Mr. Rai did not submit any formal thesis to me. Mr. Rai and I spent an hour or so discussing his ideas, which I did not find to be proven, although admittedly this is not my area of greatest expertise. As far as I know, Mr. Rai's ideas have not been published elsewhere.

Sincerely yours.
Sd/
Mark Aronoff

Professor and Chairman

This information confirmed my doubts and I was all set to make further investigations into the relationship between Sanskrit and Tuḷu. On comparing the vocabularies of Sanskrit and Tuḷu, I came to know that Tuḷu has drawn a large number of vocables from Sanskrit. A couple of them may be illustrated hereunder.

Tuḷu vocables as drawn from Sanskrit

	Tulu	**Sanskrit**
1.	Pañcakajjāyo 'a sweet preparation made with five ingredients'	*Pañcakātjāyaḥ*
2.	tāri 'tree'	*taru*
3.	paggu 'the first tuḷu month'	*phālgun*
4.	etāsti 'exact'	*yathāsthiti*
5.	kai 'hand'	*kara*
6.	ejño 'sacrifice'	*yajña*
7.	ekke 'a kind of a milk plant whose	

	flower is sacred to lord 'Śiva'	*arka*
	Tulu	**Sanskrit**
8.	batti 'stick'	*varti*
9.	kāmale 'jaundice'	*kāmalā*
10.	ūno 'deficient'	*ūna*
11.	urdi 'increase'	*vṛddhi*
12.	niru 'water'	*nārā, nīra*
13.	unguto 'the great toe'	*aṅguṣṭha*
14.	uṅgilo 'a ring'	*aṅgulīyaka*
15.	uṇasu 'a meal', 'dinner'	*aśana*
16.	utpatti 'produce'	*utpatti*
17.	upāso 'fast'	*upavāsa*
18.	udāraṇa 'example'	*udāharaṅa*
19.	kelu 'time'	*kāla*
20.	iṭṭige 'side'	*iṣṭakā*
21.	taṭṭu 'side'	*taṭa*
22.	āpattu 'calamity, illness'	*āpatti*
23.	āspāsu 'vicinity'	*āpārśva*
24.	ākāso 'sky'	*ākāśa*

Hosts of similar other examples can be cited, but the paucity of time and space restrains the present author to detail all of them here.

Eventually, on the basis of Tuḷu borrowings from Sanskrit, it can safely be observed that the prototypes of Tuḷu forms are also preserved in the Sanskrit language.

Hence, it will be more beneficial and advisable to study the history of origin and development of various Indo-European and Dravidian languages with Sanskrit as their Proto-language.

4

Evolution of the Lithuanian Language

In Vedic Language forms with radical ending ī, accept a regular ending *-au* when inflected in nominative, accusative dual. But in the Vedic language regular ending *-au* is sometimes found replaced by *-ā* and sometimes found dropped altogether. For example in the forms of *nadyā* (nom. acc. dual of *nadī*) and *yamyā* (nom. acc. dual of *yamī*) -au is found replaced by -ā, but in the forms of *rodasī, devī, bṛhatī, pṛthivī, mahī, samicī,* etc. it is found dropped altogether. (Arya, 2007: 96) The same linguistic tendency can be recorded from Lithuanian that originated from Vedic Sanskrit. Lithuanian form of *Vezamtī* is found with the radical ending *-ī* by dropping the nom. acc. dual ending. (Arya, 2007: Chapter 1, ft. 155).

Locative singular of Yuṣmad, second-person pronoun, is *tvayi* and *tve. Tve* was predominantly used in the Vedic language, whereas *tvayi* occupied a dominant place in the later Vedic and Classical Sanskrit. (Arya, 2007: 115). The Lithuanian following the pattern of Classical Sanskrit admitted *tvayi* as twiye. (Arya, 2007: Chapter 2, ft. 81)

In addition to the above-cited facts following list of borrowings in Lithuanian from Sanskrit shows its direct origin from Sanskrit, e.g.

Sanskrit	**Lithunain**
asmi (i am)	esmi
asi (you are)	essi
asti (he is)	esti
smaḥ (we are)	esmi
stha ‘second person plural (You are)	esti
paśu (animal)	penss, pecku
go (cow)	gow

Sanskrit	**Lithunain**
gau (bull)	govjado
sthura (steer)	taura-s
aśva (horse)	aszua
avi (sheep)	avi-s
makṣikā (fly)	muse
eka (numeral denoting 'one')	wein
dvau(two)	du
tri (three)	tri
catur (four)	kettuar
pañc (five)	penki
ṣaṣ (six)	szestzi
sapta (seven)	septyni
aṣṭa (eight)	asztuni
nava (nine)	dewyni
daśa (ten)	deszimt
yuvoḥ (you two)	yumu, dwieyū
(Arya : 2007: 133: fn. 106),	
yuvam (Arya 2007: 132 : fn. 87)	yudu

5

Evolution of the Avestan Language

In Vedic Language forms ending with *ī* accept a regular ending -*au* when inflected in the nominative, accusative dual. But in the Vedic language regular ending -*au* is sometimes found replaced by -*ā* and sometimes found dropped altogether. For example in the forms of *nadyā* (nom. acc. dual of nadī) and yamyā (nom. acc. dual of yamī) -*au* is found replaced by -*ā*, but in the forms of *rodasī, devī, bṛhatī, pṛthivī, mahī, samicī,* etc. it is found dropped altogether. (Arya, 2007: 96) The same linguistic tendency can be recorded from Lithuanian that originated from Vedic Sanskrit. Avestan form of *Hamoistrī* is found with the radical ending -*ī* by dropping the nom. acc. dual ending. (Arya, 2007: Chapter 1, ft. 155).

In Sanskrit, generally, the stems ending in short vowel *ṛ* admit in genitive plural a euphonic n between the normal termination -*ām* and the stem. For example*pitṛṇām* (form *pitṛ*). But in the Vedic language, we found that this insertion has been dropped in a couple of cases. For example, *narām* (in place of *nṛṇām*) occurs 16 times in the *Ṛgveda. Svasrām* occurs once in the *Ṛgveda.* (Arya, 2007: 97)The same tendency has percolated to Avesta also. There is also the insertion of euphonic n between genitive case-ending and the stem that has not been admitted. For instance, Sanskrit bhrātṛṇām becomes in Avesta as brathraṁm. (Arya, 2007: Chapter 1, ft. 161). This shows that in the earlier stages of the Vedic language, the tendency of inserting euphonic 'n' was less prevalent, but later it became more and more prevalent. Greek also exhibits the latter tendency. This proves that Greek originated from Vedic Sanskrit when the later Vedic Sanskrit was evolving.

Tyad is a pronoun that was used in the Vedic language. It became obsolete in Classical Sanskrit. (Arya, 2007: 109). The same pronoun was retained by Avesta as *thya* during the process of its evolution from Vedic Sanskrit. (Arya, 2007: Chapter 2, ft. 4)

Ava is the pronominal stem that was used scarcely even in the

Vedas. Its use is not attested in later Vedic and Classical Sanskrit. (Arya, 2007: 110) Its use is registered in Avesta as ava. (Arya, 2007: Chapter 2, ft. 11)

Locative singular of *Yuṣmad*, second-person pronoun, is *tvayi* and *tve*. *Tve* was predominantly used in the Vedic language, whereas tvayi occupied a dominant place in the later Vedic and Classical Sanskrit. (Arya, 2007 : 115) The Avesta following the pattern of Classical sanskrit admitted tvayi as thvahmi. (Arya, 2007: Chapter 2, ft. 81)

Following is list of borrowings in Avestan from Sanskrit which speaks of its origin from Sanskrit, e.g.

Sanskrit	**Avesta**
asmi (I am)	almi
asi (you Are)	ahi
asti (he is)	asti
smaḥ (we are)	hualie
stha (you are)	sta
pitṛ (father)	patar
mātṛ (mother)	matar
bhrātṛ (brother)	brator
Duhitṛ (daughter)	dighdhar
paśu (animal)	pasu
go (cow)	gao
ukṣan (bull)	ukhshan
sthura (steer)	staoru
aśva (horse)	aspa
makṣikā (fly)	makshki

In addition to the above cognates, correspondence between the following numerals (ordinal numbers) also proves that Avesta is but the corrupt form of Sanskrit only.

prathamam (first)	frat'hema
dvitīya (second)	bitya
ṭṛtīya(third)	thritya
caturtha, *turīya* (fourth)	turiya
pañcama (fifth)	pugdha
ṣaṣṭha (sixth)	cstva
saptam (seventh)	haptat'ha
aṣṭama (eighth)	astema
navam (ninth)	nauma
daśam (tenth)	dasema

The following analogy of verbs between Sanskrit and Avesta is revealing:

dad-a-mi (I give)	dadha-mi
dada-s (you give)	dadh-si
dada-te (he gives)	dadha-te
dadmaḥ (we give)	dade-mahi
dat-tha (you give)	dasta
dad-te (they give)	dade-nti

Avesta could also retain personal terminations of its source language Sanskrit while emerging as a separate language. Following examples are noteworthy :

tiṣṭhāmi (I stay)	histami
dadami (I give)	dadhami
asmi (I am)	ahmi
vahami (I carry)	vazami
bharami (I bear)	barami
asi (you are)	ahi
tiṣṭhasi (you stay)	hisht'hahi

dadasi (you give)	dadhahi
bharasi (you bear)	barahi
tiṣṭhathas (you two stay)	histois
bhares (you carry)	bharois
tiṣṭhatha (you all stay)	hist'hat'ha
bharatha (you all bear)	bara'ha
dadyāt (he should give)	daidhyata
bhareta (he should bear)	baraeta
asti (he is)	ashti
tiṣṭhati (he stays)	hishtoti
dadāti (he gives)	dadhaite
bharati (he bears)	baraite
bharet (he should bear)	baroit
dadyāt (he should give)	daidhyat
santi (they are)	hente
tiṣṭhanti (they stay)	histenti
dadati (they give)	dadenti
bharanti (they bear)	barenti
vahanti (they carry)	vazenti

The aforementioned examples prove beyond any shadow of a doubt that Avesta finds its proto-type in Sanskrit. The above fact has also been corroborated by the findings of William Jones (Sir William Jines' works, Vol.1, pp.82-83) following remarks. he says, 'I was not little surprised to find that out of ten words in Du Peron's Zind Dictionary six or seven out of ten words were pure Sanskrit.' In view of the above fact, Prof. Heeren (Historical Researches, Vol. ī, p.20) had to declare that 'In point of fact, the Zind is derived from Sanskrit.' Thus the affinity of European languages and Old Parsi with Sanskrit and the use of cognate idioms by these languages proves that the nations who used them must have descended from Indian stock.

6

Evolution of the Greek Language

In Sanskrit, generally the stems ending in short vowel *'ṛ'* admit in genitive plural a euphonic *'n'* between the normal termination -*ām* and the stem. For example*pitṛṇām* (form *pitṛ*). But in the Vedic language, we found that this insertion has been dropped in a couple of cases. For example, *narām* (in place of *nṛṇām*) occurs 16 times in the *Ṛgveda*. *Svasrām* occurs once in the *Ṛgveda*. (Arya, 2007: 97). The same tendency has percolated to Greek also. There is also the insertion of euphonic '*n*' between genitive case-ending and the stem has been admitted and the genitive case-ending -*ām*has been admitted as -on (ωυ). For instance, Sanskrit *bhrātṛṇām* becomes in Greek as παιερωυ. (Arya, 2007: Part 2, Chapter 1, ft. 161). This shows that in the earlier stages of the Vedic language, the tendency of inserting euphonic 'n' was less prevalent, but later it became more and more prevalent. Greek also exhibits the latter tendency. This proves that Greek originated from Vedic Sanskrit when the later Vedic Sanskrit was evolving.

Although students of both Greek and Latin may be impressed with their similarities, Latin does not have a dual number, a middle voice, or an aorist tense, which both Greek and Sanskrit share. These features, and others, prove that Latin originated from Sanskrit very late as compared to Greek.

Following are some of the borrowings in Greek from Sanskrit which speaks of its origin from Sanskrit, e.g.

Sanskrit	**Greek**	**Meaning in English**
1. *tānam*	tonom	tone
2. *paru*	pur	fire
3. *pardate*	bdeetai	farteth (fart)
4. *puras*	paros	fore
5. *fullam*	phullon	flower
6. *phavate*	phvetai	beeth,

Sanskrit	Greek	Meaning in English
7. *bhrū*	ophrus	brow
8. *madhu*	methu	mead
9. *manate*	mnaetai	meaneth
10. *mahatva*	megethos	might
11. *me*	me	me
12. *roṣa*	orgç	rage
13. *rohita*	ereuthon	red
14. *vakṣate*	aezetai	waxeth
15. *vepate*	uphaetai	weaveth
16. *śāla*	skholç	school
17. *hanum*	genuu	chin
18. *ajra 'plain'*	ager	acre, agriculture
19. *trikoṇamiti*	trigonov	trignometry
20. *takṣaka*	töeikhov	tonic
21. *ātma, aṇu*	atomas	atom
22. *amṛta*	immortal	immortle

7

Evolution of the Latin

In Sanskrit, generally, the stems ending in short vowel *ṛ* admit in genitive plural a euphonic n between the normal termination -ām and the stem. For example*pitṛṇām*(form *pitṛ*). But in the Vedic language, we found that this insertion has been dropped in a couple of cases. For example, narām (in place of nṛṇām) occurs 16 times in the *Ṛgveda. Svasrām* occurs once in the Ṛgveda. (Arya, 2007: 97)The same tendency has percolated to Latin also. There is also the insertion of euphonic n between genitive case-ending and the stem has not been admitted and the genitive case-ending -ām has been admitted as -um. For instance, Sanskrit *bhrātṛṇām*becomes in Latin as fratr-um. (Arya, 2007: Part, 2 Chapter 1, ft. 161). This shows that in the earlier stages of the Vedic language, the tendency of inserting euphonic '*n*' was less prevalent, but later it became more and more prevalent. Greek also exhibits the latter tendency. This proves that Greek originated from Vedic Sanskrit when the later Vedic Sanskrit was evolving.

Locative singular of *yuṣmad*, second-person pronoun, is tvayi and tve. *Tve* was predominantly used in the Vedic language, whereas tvayi occupied a dominant place in the later Vedic and Classical Sanskrit. (Arya, 2007: 115) Latin following the pattern of Classical Sanskrit admitted *tvayi* as *tvi.* (Arya, 2007: Chapter 2, ft. 81)

Latin does not have a dual number, a middle voice, or an aorist tense, which both Greek and Sanskrit share. These features, and others, prove that Latin indirectly originated from Vedic Sanskrit very late as compared to Greek.

The following list of borrowings in Latin from Sanskrit also speaks of Latin's origin from Sanskrit, e.g.

Sanskrit	Latin	Meaning in English
1. *tarman*	terminus	term
2. *tānam*	tonum	tone
3. *naddham*	nodum	knot

Sanskrit	Latin	Meaning in English
4. *pardate*	pedit	farteth (fart)
5. *puras*	prae	fore
6. *prānta*	frontem	front
7. *fullam*	folium	flower
8. *phavate*	fuit	beeth
9. *manate*	monet	meaneth
10. *me*	me	me
11. *mitam*	metitum	meted
12. *mṛtam*	mortuum	mortal
13. *yat*	id	it
14. *yuvan*	juvenis	young
15. *lapana*	labium	lip
16. *locayati*	lucet	lixeth (A.S.)
17. *vakṣate*	auget	waxeth
18. *varāhaḥ*	verses	boar,bare (A.S.)
19. *vastyayati*	vastat	wasteth
20. *śāla*	schola	school
21. *śṛnga*	cornu	horn
22. *santaḥ*	sanctus	saint
23. *siwati*	suit	seweth
24. *sīdati*	cedet	cedeth
25. *svanitam*	sonitum	sound

8

Evolution of Old Slav. and other Slavic languages

Locative singular of *yuṣmad*, second-person pronoun, is *tvayi* and *tve*. *Tve* was predominantly used in the Vedic language, whereas *tvayi* occupied a dominant place in the later Vedic and Classical Sanskrit. (Arya, 2007: 115) Old Slav. following the pattern of Classical Sanskrit admitted *tvayi* as 'tebye'. (Arya, 2007: Chapter 2, ft. 81). In addition to this, Slavic languages evolved the comparison of the following Slavic terms with that of Sanskrit gives one to understand the deep-rooted relationship of Slavic languages with Sanskrit and

Following borrowings in Slavic languages from Sanskrit speaks of their origin from Sanskrit, e.g.

Sanskrit	Meaning in English	Slovenian	Czech	Russian
Words associated with water, moisture and other liquids				
megha	cloud	Megla	mlha (fog)	mgla (gloom)
Mṛṣ, marṣati	to sprinkle, pour out	Mr"éati	mziti	marasit'
pa, papīyat	to quaff, drink intox. Liquors	Popivati	popijeti	zapit'
pa, pāyayati	cause to drink	Pojiti	(na)pájet i	poit'
pa, pibati	to drink, quaff	Piti	pîti	pit'
Phena	foam, froth, saliva	Pena	pína	Pena

Piti	drinking	Pitje	pitî	pit'io
plavana	swimming, floating	Plavanje	plavánî	plavan'e
plu, plavate	to swim, float	Plavati	plavati	plavat'

Sanskrit	**Meaning in English**	**Slovenian**	**Czech**	**Russian**
Rasa	moisture, humidity, any liquid	rosa (dew)	rosa	rosa (dew)
salilavat	provided with water	Zalivan	zalîvan	Zalityy
sarasa	a lake, pond	Jezero	jezero	Ozero
sna, snasyati	to bathe, wash, cleanse	Snaßiti	x	X
uda,am	water	voda (also: uda)	voda	Voda
voda, udanya	moist	Voden	vodnî	X
varṣ &pruṣ ṇoti	to rain, shower down	Pr“iti	pr“eti	marasit'
apuplavat	to inundate, to submerge	Poplaviti	zaplaviti	
Varya	watery, aquatic	barje, bara		

Words associated with food, food preparation and consumption

ad, atsyati	to eat	jesti	jîsti	yest'
adanīya	to be	jeden	jîdlo	s'ieden

	eaten, what may be eaten			
Adya	food	jed	jîdlo	yeda
cuṣati	to suck	cuzati, sesati	cucati	sosat'
cuṣana	sucking	cuzanje	cucánî	sosanie'
Dhe, dhayati	to give suck, nourish	dojiti	dojiti (animal)	doit'
gavyaya	coming from cattle	goveje	hovadina	goviadina
gavyayayu ṣa	beef soup	govejajuha	x	goviazhiayu shka
ghas,-ati	to consume or devour, eat	gostiti se, kositi	pásti se (graze)?	x
Ghasi	food	Kaša	x	kasha

Sanskrit	**Meaning in English**	**Slovenian**	**Czech**	**Russian**
Ghasa	food, meadow or pasture grass	Koša	kosení	X
Jeh, jehate	be thirsty; to open the mouth	žejati; zehati, zevati	žíznit	zhazhdat'; zevat
Jivatu	victuals, food	Živež	x	X

kośa, koṣ a	vessel, box, bucket, store-room	koš, košara	koš	Kovsh
koṣṭaka	granary, store-room	Kašèa	x	X
Kṣīra	milk, thickened milk	sir (cheese)	syr	syr (cheese)
kuṣ,-ati; kuṣ,-ṇāti	to gnaw, nibble; to test	(po)kušati ; skušati	pokoštov ati:skouš etskoušet	kushat'; x
Mas	flesh, meat; month	meso; mesec	maso: mesíc	miaso; miesiats
mekṣaṇa	stick or spoon for stirring	Mešalka	méchaèk a	Meshalka
mikṣ, mekṣayati	to stir up, mix, mingle	Mešati	míchatí	meshat'
pa, pibati/ papīyat	to drink	Piti	pítí	pit'
pac-ati	to bake, cook	Peèi	peèi	pech'
pacana	cooking, roasting	Peèenje	peèeni	Pechenyi
Paktri	one who bakes or roasts	Pek	pekaø	pekar'
pāpacyate	to cook very much, burn	Popeèi	pøepéci	popech'

Sanskrit	Meaning in English	Slovenian	Czech	Russian
papīti	mutual or reciprocal drinking	popivanje	popíjení	x
pīta	food, nourishment	pièa	x	pishcha
Pita	saturated, filled with	pitan	x	napitan
pūrṇa	Filled, full, abundant	poln	plny	polon, polnyi
sūpa	soup, broth	župa	x	sup
yemana= jemana	Eating	jemati (zdravilo)	x	x

Words associated with death, pain and pleasure

bal,-ate	to hurt; to expound	boleti	boleti	bolet'
bharts-ayati	to abuse, to pain	brcati	x	
du, davayati	to cause pain, sorrow	daviti	x	davit'(to press)
kaṣ-ati	to scrape, hurt, destroy	kaziti	kazit	kaznit'(execute)
klath-ati	To hurt, kill	klati	x	kolot'
Kṛcchara	causing trouble, pain	krè (cramp)	x	x

krudha	harsh, cruel	krut	kruty	x
Kruś, krośati	to cry out, shriek	krièati	krièet	krichat'
math-ati	to trouble, disturb	motiti	x	mutit'
mṛ, maryate	to kill, slay	moriti	x	morit'
mṛ, mriyate/ marate	to die, decease	mreti, umirati	umirat	umirat'
mṛc, marcayati	to hurt, injure	mrcvariti	x	x

Sanskrit	**Meaning in English**	**Slovenian**	**Czech**	**Russian**
Mṛta	dead, rigid, torpid	Mrtev	mrtevt	Miortv
Mṛyu	dying, death	mrtje=mr etje, smrt	umirati, smrt	sm'ert'
Mṛtaka	dead man, corpse	Mrtvak	mrtvola, mrtvelec	m'ertv'ets
pratap-ayati	to destroy, torment	Pretepati	trapit	X
ru, rauti	to roar, cry outloud	Rjuti	rvat	orat'

ru, ravate	to break, kill	Ruvati	x	rubit'
rup, ropayat	to cause violent pain	ropati (plunder)	x	X
ruṣ,-ati	to hurt, injure, kill	rušiti (destroy)	rušit	rushit (destroy)
vraṇ,ati	to wound	Raniti	ranit	ranit'
vraṇa	Wound	Rana	rana	Rana
vunt-ayati	to kill, hurt	Fentati	x	X
Verb 'to be'				
Asmi	I am	Sem	jsem	X; yesm' (archaic) (archaic0 (archaic)
Asi	you are	Si	jsi	X; yesi (archaic)
Asti	he, she, it is	x (je)	x (je)	Yest
svaḥ	X	Sva	x	X
sthaḥ	X	sta	x	X
staḥ	X	Sta	x	X
smaḥ	we are	smo	jsme	X; (yest)
Stha	you are	Ste	jste	X; (yest)
Santi	they are	x (so)	x (jsou)	X; (yest)
Numerals				
Eka	One	eden:nek (someone) (neki) (someone)	néjaký (someone)	Odin

Sanskrit	**Meaning in English**	**Slovenian**	**Czech**	**Russian**
dvi (dva)	Two	Dva	dva	dva
Tri	Three	Tri	tøi	tri
Catur	Four	štiri (èetveri)	ètýøi	chetyre
pañc	Five	pet	pét	piat'
ṣaṣ, ṣaṭ	Six	Šest	šest	shest'
Saptan	Seven	sedem	sedm	siem'
Aṣṭan	Eight	osem	osm	vasiem'
Navan	Nine	devet	devét	dieviat'
daśan	Ten	deset	deset	diesiat'
ekādaśan	Eleven	enajst	jedenáct	odinnadsat'
Dvadaśan	Twelve	dvanajst	dvananáct	dvenadsat'
śata	hundred	Sto	sto	sut', sto

From the above comparison, it can be seen that Slovenian has preserved a more general vocabulary of Sanskrit than other Slavic languages such as Czech and Russian that is common to Sanskrit. In some cases, Slovenian still preserves vocabulary and grammatical forms no longer used in Indian languages such as Hindi and Punjabi. The conjugation of the verb *to be* is a good example.

Slovenian has also kept the meaning of the words quite close to the Vedic Sanskrit, along with the sounds. The greatest similarity is with the Vedic Sanskrit - the language of the Vedas.

9

Sanskrit Origin of Numbers in the World Languages

Numerals in all the world languages find their origin directly or indirectly from Sanskrit. Following comparison of numerals of world languages with that of Sanskrit proves this fact.

Chart 1 (Numerals from No.1 to No.5)

Languages	No.1	No. 2	No.3	No.4	No.5
Indo European					
Sanskrit	ekaÌ/ ekas	dvau	trayas	catvÈraÌ/ catvaras	*pa¤-ca
Germanic					
Old Germanic+	*ainaz	*twai	*thrijiz	*fithwor	*fimfi
Western					
Old English+	án	twá	þrí	féower	fíf
Middle English+	an	two	three	four	fif
English	one	two	three	four	five
Scots	ane	twa	thrie	fower	fyve
Old Frisian+	en	twe	thre	fiuwer	fif
W.Frisian	ien	twa	trije	fjouwer	fiif
Frisian (Saterland)	aan	twæi	træi	fjauer	fieuw
Dutch	een	twee	drie	vier	vijf
W/S Flemish	ièn	twiè	drie	viere	vuvve
Brabants	iën	twië	draë	vi:r	vaëf
Low Saxon	een	twee	dree	veer	fief
Emsland	*e*in	tw*e*i	dr*e*i	fe*i*æ	fi:f
Mennonite	een	twee	dree	fea	Fief

Plautdietsch					
Afrikaans	een	twee	drie	vier	vyf
German	eins	zwei	drei	vier	fünf
Central Bavarian	oans	zwoa	drai	viare	fimbfe
Swabian	oes	zwoe	droe	vier	fümf
Alsatian	eins	zwei	drëi	vier	fenf
Cimbrian	òan	zbeen	drai	viar	vüf
Rimella	ais	zwai	drei	viére	venve
Rheinfränkisch	ääns	zwei	drej	vir	fennef
Pennsylvania	eens	zwee	drei	vier	fimf
Luxembourgeois	eent	zwee	dräi	véier	fënnef
Swiss German	eis	zwei	drüü	vier	foif
Yiddish	eyns	tsvey	dray	fir	finef
Middle High German+	ein	zwe:ne	dri:e	vier	fünf
Old High German+	ein	zwâ	drî	fior	fimf
Northern					
Runic+	æinn	tvæiR	þri:R	fiu:riR	fæ:m
Old Norse+	einn	tveir	thrír	fjórir	fimm
Norwegian	en (*Ny.*ein)	to	tre	fire	fem
Danish	én	to	tre	fire	fem
Swedish	en	två	tre	fyra	fem
Faroese	ein	tveir	tríggir	fy'ra	fimm
Old Icelandic+	einn	tueir	þrír	fiórer	fimm
Icelandic	einn	tveir	þrír	fjórir	fimm
Eastern					
Gothic+	ains	twai	þreis	fidwor	fimf
Crimean+	ene	tua	tria	fyder	fyuf

Italic					
Oscan+	uinus	dus	tris	petora	pompe-
Umbrian+	uns	tuf	trif	petur-	pumpe-
Faliscan+		du	tris		*cuicue
Latin+	u:nus	duo	tre:s	quattuor	quinque
Romance					
Mozarabic+	uno	dox	trex	quatro	chinco
Portuguese	um	dois	três	quatro	cinco
Galician	un	dous	tres	catro	cinco
Spanish	uno	dos	tres	cuatro	cinco
Ladino	unu	do	tre	cuatru	sincu
Asturian	uno	dos	tres	cuatru	cincu
Aragonese	un	dos	tres	cuatro	zinco
Catalan	un	dos	tres	quatre	cinc
Valencian	u	dos	tres	quatre	cinc
Old French+	un	deus	treis	quatre	cinc
French	un	deux	trois	quatre	cinq
Walloon	onk	deus	troes	cwate	cénk
Jèrriais	ieune	deux	trais	quat'	chînq
Poitevin	in	deùs	tràes	quatre	cénc
Old Picard+	ung	diaus	trois	katre	chincq
Picard	in	deu	trouo	kat	chink
Occitan (Provençal)	un	dos	tres	quatre	cinc
Lengadocian	un	dos	tres	quatre	cinc
Gascon	un	dus	tres	quate	cinc
Auvergnat	vun	dou	trei	catre	sin
Limosin	un	do:u:	trei	qua:tre	cin
Franco-Provençal (Vaudois)	on	doû	trâi	quatro	cin

RumantschGrisc hun	in	dus	trais	quatter	tschintg
Sursilvan	in	dus	treis	quater	tschun
Vallader	ün	duos	trais	quatter	tschinch
Friulian	u~ng	doy	tre	kwàtri	chingk
Ladin	un	doi	trëi	cater	cinc
Dalmatian+	join	doi	tra	kwatro	chenk
Italian	uno	due	tre	quattro	cinque
Piedmontese	ün	Dü	trè	quatr	sinc
Milanese	vun	duu	trii	quatter	cinqu
Genovese	un	doì	trei	quattro	çinque
Venetian	on	Do	tri	cuatro	sinque
Parmesan	von	Du	trì	cuatar	sinc
Corsican	unu	dui	trè	quattru	cinque
Umbrian	unu	dui	tre	quattru	cénque
Neapolitan	unë	rujë	tréië	quattë	cinghë
Sicilian	unu	dui	**tr**i	qua**tt**ru	cincu
Romanian	unu	doi	trei	patru	cinci
Arumanian	unu	doi	trei	patru	**t**in**t**i
Meglenite	unu	doi	trei	patru	**t**in**t**i
Istriot	ur	doi	trei	påtru	**t**in**t**
Sardinian	unu	duos	tres	báttor	chimbe
Celtic					
Proto-Celtic+	oinos	dvai	treis	qetveres	qenqe
Gaulish+	*ônos	*duô	treis	petor	*pempe
Brythonic (P-Celtic)					
Welsh	un	dau	tri	pedwar	pump
Cardiganshire	în	Tô	târ	câr	cw^i
Breton	unan	daou	tri	pewar	pemp

Vannetais	unan	deu	tri	pear	pemp
Unified Cornish+	un	deu	try	peswar	pymp
Common	onan	dew	tri	peswar	pymp
Modern	on	deaw	try	pager	pemp
Devonian+	un	deu	tri	peduar	pemp
Goidelic (Q-Celtic)					
Old Irish+	óen	da	tri	ceth(a)ir	cóic
Irish	aon	dó	trí	ceathair	cúig
Scots Gaelic	aon	dà	trì	ceithir	cóig
Manx	nane	jees	tree	kiore	queig
Hellenic					
Mycenean Greek+	e-me (*hemei)	du-wo (*dwo)	ti-ri- (*tri-)	qe-to-ro (*q^{u}etro-)	
Classical Greek+	hei:s	dúo:	trei:s	téttares	pénte
Greek	éna	dhío	tría	téssera	pénde
Cypriot	énas	thkió	dris	désseris	bénde
Tsakonian	éna	dhíu	chía	tésera	pénde
Tocharian					
Tocharian A+	sas	wu	tre	s'twar	päñ
Tocharian B+	se	wi	trai	s'twer	pis'
Albanian					
Albanian	një	dy	tre	katër	pesë
Gheg (Qosaj)	n'â	dy	tre	katër	pês
Tosk (Mandritsa)	ni	g'u	tri	kátrë	pésë
Armenian					
+Classical Armenian	mi	erk'u	erek^{h}	chork^{h}	hing
Baltic					

West					
Old Prussian+	ai:ns	dwa:i	trijan	keturja:i	pe:nkja:i
East					
Lithuanian	víenas	dù	try~s	Keturì	penkì
Latvian	viêns	divi	trî:s	Chetri	pìeci
Latgalian	vi:ns	divi	trejs	Chetri	pi:ci
Slavic					
East					
Russian	odín odín	dva dva	tri tri	ceti:re chety're	pÁth pyat'
Belarussian	adzín adzín	dva dva	try try	cati:ry chaty'ry	pÁthh piac'
Ukrainian	odín ody'n	dva dva	tri tri	Cotíri choty'ry	p'Áth pyat'
West					
Polish	jeden	dwa	trzy	Cztery	pie,c'
Kashubian	jeden	dva	tr^ë	shtërë	pjin'c
Polabian+	janü	dåvo	tåri	citêr	pa,t
Czech	jeden	dva	tr^i	chtyr^i	pêt
Slovak	jeden	dva	tri	shtyri	pät'
West	jeden	dva	try	shtyry	pet
East	jeden	dva	tri	shtyri	pejc
Upper Sorbian	jedyn	dwaj	tr^i	shtyri	pjec'
Lower Sorbian	jaden	dwa	ts'o	styrjo	pês'
South					
Old Church Slavonic+	jedinu	diva	trije	chetyre	pe,ti
Bulgarian	edín	dva	tri	chétiri	pet
Macedonian	eden	dva	tri	chetiri	pet
Serbo-Croat	jèdan	dvâ	trî	chètiri	pêt

Slovene	ena	dva	tri	shtiri	pet
Anatolian					
Hittite+	*a:nt-	da:-	tri-	meiu-	
Luwian+	*a-	duwa-	*tarri-	*mawi-	*pa^{n}ku
Lycian+	sñta	tuwa	tri(ja)	teteri	
Indo-Iranian					
Iranian					
Eastern					
Ossetian Iron	iu	dIuuæ	ærtæ	tsIppar	fondz
Digor	ieu	duuæ	ærtæ	cuppar	fondz
Avestan+	ae:uua-	duua	thra:iio:	chathBa: ro:	pancha
Khwarezmian+	'yw	dhw	shy	cf'r	pnc
Sogdian+	'yw		dhry	chtf'r	panch
Yaghnobi	i:	du	siráu	tafó:r	panch
Bactrian+	io:go			sofaro	
Saka+	s's'au	duva	drai	tcahora	pa**m**jsa
Pashto	yaw	dwa	dre	tsalór	pindz^{é}
Wakhi	i:	bu	tru	cybyr	pa:nz^{j}
Munji	yu	lu	sherai	chfu:r	pa:nj
Yidgha	yu	loh	shuroi	chshi:r	panj
Ishkashmi	uk	di,	ru,	ci,fu,r	pu,ndz
Sanglechi	vak	do:u	tra:i	safo:r	panz
Shughn	yi:w	dhu	aráy	cavó:r	pi:ndz
Rushani	yi:w	dhaw	aráy	cavú,r	pi:ndz
Yazgulami	wu,	dhow	cu,y	cher	penj
Sarikoli (Tashkorghani)	iw	dhew	aróy	cavúr	pindz
Parachi	zhu	Di	shi	cho:r	po:nc
Ormuri	so:	dyo:	sh.^{r}e:	tsa:r	pe:ndz

Western

Northwest

Parthian+	'yw	dw		cf'r	pnj
Yazdi	ya	Du	sey	chuhr	pänj
Nayini	yak			cha:or	penj
Natanzi	yæk	Do	se	chahar	pänj
Khunsari	yäg	Dô:	se	cha:r	pe:sh
Gazi	yeg	Dü	se	cha:r	ba:ng^
Sivandi	yä	Do	se	cha:r	päng^
Vafsi	yey	Do	se	caar	pezh
Semnani	i	Do	hejrá	cha:r	panj
Sangisari	yækæ'	d^{o}o	shæ	chår	panj
Gilaki	y^{e}k	Du	se	chår	p^{e}nj
Mazanderani	yak	De	se	cha:r	panj
Talysh	i	Du	se	cho	penj
Harzani	i	De	here	chö	pinch
Zaza	zhew	Di	hi:re:	chihaa:r	pa:nzh
Gorani	yak	d'ue	y'are	chu'a:r	panj
Baluchi	y^{e}k	Do	s^{e}h	car	p^{e}nj
Turkmenistan	yak	Du	say	cha:r	panch
Eastern Hill	yak	Do	sai	chiár	phanch
Rakhshani (Western)	y^{e}kk	dw	s^{e}y	char	p^{e}nch
Kermanji (S) Kurdish	yak	Du:	se:	chwa:r	pe:nj
Zaza (N) Kurdish	e:k	Dô	se:	cha:r	pe:nj
Bajalani	ikke:	Du:wa	sa	chwa:r	panj
Kermanshahi	yäkî'	dû'an	sî'an	chuâr	Pänch

South west

Old Persian+	aiva				*pancha

Pahlavi+	e:vak	do:	si:	chaha:r	panch
Farsi	yak	do	se	chaha:r	panj
Isfahani	ye(k)	do	se	tsâr	payn
Tajik	yak	du	se	chor	panj
Tati	yæ	dy"	sæ	char	panj
Chali	i	dö	sö	cua:r	panj
Fars	yek	do	se	chår	pänj
Lari	yak	do	se	ca:r	panj
Luri	ya	du	se	cha:r	panch
Kumzari	yek	doh	soh	cha:r	panj
Nuristani					
Ashkun	ach	d**o:**	trä	cata:	p**o:**nc
Wasi-weri	ipü:n	lü:	cshi:	ch^{i}pu:	wuchu
Kati	ev	d'u	tre	sht^{e}vo	puch
Kalasha-ala	ew	dü:	tre:	chata:	pu:~
Indic					
Prakrit+	ekko:	do:	tao:	chatta:ri	pañcha
Ardhamagadhi+	ege	do	tao	cattaro	pa**m**ca
Pali+	eka	dvi	ti	catu	pañca
Romany (Gypsy)					
Spanish	yes	duis	trin	sistar	parchen
Welsh	yek'	du:i:	trin	shto:r	pansh
Kalderash	yek(h)	duy	trin	shtar	panz'
Syrian	e:kâ	di:	târân	shta:r	Panj
Armenian	jäku	du:^{i}	t^{e}rín	ishdó:r	Bench
Iranian	yek	duy	terín	Ishta:r	pa:nj

Sinhalese-Maldivian					
Sinhalese	eka	deka	tuna	hatara	Paha
Vedda	ekamay	dekamay	tunamay	hataramay	pahamay
Maldivian	eke	de	tine	hatare	Fahe
Northern India					
Dardic					
Kashmiri	akh	zɨ	tr'ɨ	co:r	pa:nc
Shina	êk	du	**ch**e	char	poi~
Brokskat	e:k	du	tra	ch^{h}or	Puns
Phalura	a:k	du:	tro:	chu:r	pa:nzh
Bashkarik	ak	du:	**t**ha:	cho:r	Panj
Tirahi	ek	do:	tre	cawo:r	Panc
Torwali	ek	du	cha	chau	Pan
Wotapuri	yek	du:	**t**a:	cawu:r	Panzh
Maiya	ak	du:	**t**ha:	saur	pa:nz
Kalasha	ek	du	tre	chau	P**oñ**
Khowar	i	ju	troy	chhor	Ponj
Dameli	ek	du:	trâ	cho:r	pâ~ch
Gawar-bati	yok	du:	l^{y}e	cu:r	po:nc
Pashai	i:	do:	trä	cha:r	Panja
Shumashti	yäk	du:	l^{y}y	cöuur	po:n
Nangalami	yak	du:	**sl**e:	ch^{u}or	Pa**n**
Dumaki	ek	dui	**c**ai	chouur	Poi
Western					
Marathi	ek	don	ti:n	char	pac
Konkani	êk	dôn	tin	char	panch
Sindhi	hiku	bba	**t**i:	ca:re	pañja
Khatri	hakro	bo	trê	chár	panj

Lahnda	hikk	do:e:	trä	cha:r	pañ
Central					
Hindi/ Urdu	ek	do	ti:n	ca:r	pã:c
Parya	yek	do	tin	char	panj
Punjabi	yk	do	tyn	car	p^{e}ñj
Siraiki	hik	du	tre	ca:r	pañj
Gujarati	ek	be	tr^{e}ñ	car	pãc
Rajasthani (Marwari)	e:k	do:y	ti:n	chya:r	pã:ch
Banjari (Lamani)	ek	di	tin	caar	paanc
Malvi	e:k	do:	ti:n	cha:r	pã:ch
Bhili	e:k	be:	te:n.	sya:r	pã:s
Dogri	ik	do:	trai	cha:r	pañj
Kumauni	e:k	dwi:	ti:n	cha:r	pã:ch
Garhwali	e:k	dwi:	ti:n	cha:r	pã:ch
W Pahari	e:k	dui	co:n	tsa:r	pa:ndz
Khandeshi	e:k	do:n	ti:n	cha:r	pa:ch
East Central					
Nepali	ek	dui	tin	cha:r	pa:nch
Maithili	ek	du:	ti:n	cha:ri	pã:ch
Magahi	ek	du:	ti:n	ca:r	pa:ñc
Bhojpuri	e:k	dui	ti:n	ca:ri	pã:c
Awadhi (Kosali)	e:k	dui	ti:ni	ca:ri	pã:c
Chattisgarhi	e:k	dui	ti:n	cha:r	pã:ch
Eastern					
Oriya	ek	du'i	tini	chaari	paanjch
Bengali	æk	dui	tin	car	Pãc
Assamese	ek	dui	tini	sari	Pãs
Mayang	a:	du:	tin	sa:ri	pa:z

Elamite					
Elamite+	Ki	--	atbazash		
Northwest					
Brahui	Asi	Ira:	musi	cha:r	Panch
Northeast					
Kurukh	O**nt**a:	e**mr**	mu:nd	na:kh	pance:
Malto	Ort	irw	ti:ne	ca:re	pa:ce
Central					
Kolami	okkod	i:ral	muyal	nallav	Seyyav
Naiki	okko	iro**t**el	muggur	nalgur	
Parji	o:kuri:	irul	mu:ir	nilir	se:vir
Gadaba	okur	iruvul	muvur	naluvur	aydu-gur
Telugu	oka**t**i	re**nd**u	muu**d**u	naalugu	Aydu
Gondi	undi:	rend	mu:nd	na:lu:ng	siya:ng
Koya	orro	re**nd**u	mu:n.**d**u	na:lu	a:y**d**u
Konda	unr̲i	ru**nd**i	mu:nr̲i	na:lgi	Aydu
Manda	ru	ri		l**a**lur	Seyyur
Pengo	ro	ri	tin	car	Pãc
Kui	ro	ri	muñji	na:lgi	Singgi
Kuvi	ro:ndi	rindi	ti:ni	sa:ri	pa:sa
South					
Tulu	onji	radd	mu:ji	na:l	Ein
Koraga	onji	raddi	muji	nali	ayni
Kannada	ondu	eraDu	muuru	naaku	aydu
Badaga	ondu	era**d**u	mu:ru	na:ku	aidu
Kodagu	ond^{ü}	dan**d**^{ü}	mu:nd^{ü}	na:t^{ü}	anji
Kurumba	-o**nd**e	-^{e}ddu	-mu.r̲ʉ̲	-na.kʉ̲	-^{e}yidʉ̲
Toda	wï**d**	e:d	mu:d	no:ng	üz,
Kota	vodde	yede	mu:nde	na:ke	anje

Tamil	onrru	eranndu	moonrru	naanku	i:ynthu
Malayalam	onnu	ra**nt**u	mu:nnu	na:lu	ancu
Irula	vondu	irndu	mura	na:ku	eindu
Nahali					
Nahali	bi**d**um	irar	mo**t**ho	na:lo	pãco
Burushashki					
Hunza	hik	altó	iskí	wálti	cshindí
Yasin	hek	altó	iskí	wálte	cendí
Basque					
Ancient Basque+	*bade	*biga	*(h)ilur	*laur	*bortz(e)
Basque	bat	bi	hiru	lau	bost
Etruscan					
Etruscan	thu(n)	zal	ci	huth	mach
Hurrian					
Hurrian	--	shin	kig	tumni	---
Meroitic					
Meroitic	--	tbu	---	---	---

Chart 2 (Numerals from No.6 to No.10)

Languages	No.6	No. 7	No.8	No.9	No.10
Vedic or					
Indo European					
Sanskrit	*ṣaṭa*	*sapta*	*aṣṭa/ aṣṭau*	*navam*	*daśam*
Germanic					
Old Germanic+	*seks	*sibum	*ahto:	*niwun	*tehun
Western					
Old English+	sex	seofon	eahta	nighon	Tíen
Middle English+	six	seven	eihte	nien	Ten
English	six	seven	eight	nine	Ten
Scots	sax	seiven	aicht	nyne	Ten
Old Frisian+	sex	sigun	achta	nigun	Tian
W.Frisian	seis	sân	acht	njoggen	Tsien
Frisian (Saterland)	sæks	sogen	oachte	njugen	Tjoon
Dutch	zes	zeven	acht	negen	Tien
W/S Flemish	zèsse	ze:vne	achte	ne:gne	Tiene
Brabants	zes	ze:ve	acht	ne:ge	Ting
Low Saxon	söß	söven	acht	negen	Teihn
Emsland	zes	ze:bm	axt	ne:ng	Tain
Mennonite Plautdietsch	sass	säwen	acht	näajen	Tian
Afrikaans	ses	sewe	agt	nege	Tien
German	sechs	sieben	acht	neun	Zehn
Central Bavarian	sechse	simme	aochte	naine	Zene
Swabian	sechs	siibe	acht	noen	Zaen
Alsatian	sex	seve	acht	nin	Zehn

Cimbrian	sèks	siban	acht	naün	Zègan
Rimella	zhakshe	shìbne	achtwe	nine	Zìne
Rheinfränkisch	sechs	siwe	acht	nin	Zeen
Pennsylvania	sex	siwwe	acht	nein(e)	Zeh
Luxembourgeois	sechs	siwen	aacht	néng	Zéng
Swiss German	sächs	siebë	acht	nüün	Zäh
Yiddish	zeks	zibn	akht	nayn	Tsen
Middle High German+	sëhs	siben	ahte	niun	Zëhen
Old High German+	sehs	sibun	ahto	niun	Zehan
Northern					
Runic+	sæx	siu:	a:tta	ni:u	ti:u
Old Norse+	sex	sjau	átta	níu	tíu
Norwegian	seks	sju	åtte	ni	ti
Danish	seks	syv	otte	ni	ti
Swedish	sex	sju	åtta	nio	tio
Faroese	seks	sjey	átta	níggju	tíggju
Old Icelandic+	sex	siau	átta	nío	tío
Icelandic	sex	sjö	átta	níu	tíu
Eastern					
Gothic+	saíhs	sibun	ahtau	niun	taíhun
Crimean+	seis	sevene	athe	nyne	thiine
Italic					
Oscan+	*sehs	*seften	*uhto	*nuven	*deken
Umbrian+	sehs-			*nuvim	*desem
Faliscan+	zex	*zepte n	octu	*neuen	
Latin+	sex	septem	octo:	novem	decem
Romance					

Mozarabic+	xaix	xebte	oito	(nove)	diex
Portuguese	seis	sete	oito	nove	dez
Galician	seis	sete	oito	nove	dez
Spanish	seis	siete	ocho	nueve	Diez
Ladino	sex	sieti	ochu	muevi	Dies
Asturian	seis	siete	ochu	nueve	Diez
Aragonese	seis	siet	güeito	nueu	Diez
Catalan	sis	set	vuit	nou	Deu
Valencian	sis	set	huit	nou	Deu
Old French+	sis	set	oit	nous	Dis
French	six	sept	huit	neuf	Dix
Walloon	shijh	set	ût	noûf	Dijh
Jèrriais	six	sept	huit	neuf	Dgix
Poitevin	sis	sét	uit	neùv	Dis
Old Picard+	sies	siet	wict	niuf	Deis
Picard	sis	siet	uit	neuf	Dich
Occitan (Provençal)	sièis	sèt	vuèch	nòu	Dètz
Lengadocian	sièis	sèt	uèch	nòu	Dètz
Gascon	shèis	sèt	ueit	nau	Dètz
Auvergnat	siei	sé	veu	neu	Dié
Limosin	siei	se	hue	no:	Die
Franco-Provençal (Vaudois)	sî	sat	houit	nâo	Dyî
RumantschGrischun	sis	set	otg	nov	Diesch
Sursilvan	sis	siat	otg	nov	Diesch
Vallader	ses	set	ot	nuov	Desch
Friulian	sîs	syet	vot	nûf	Dîs
Ladin	síes	set	òt	nuéf	Díesc

Dalmatian+	si	sapto	guapto	nu	Dik
Italian	sei	sette	otto	nove	Dieci
Piedmontese	sés	sèt	öt	nöu	Dés
Milanese	sés	sètt	vòtt	noeuv	Dés
Genovese	sei	sette	euttu	neuve	Dexe
Venetian	sié	sete	oto	nove	Diese
Parmesan	s*e*:s	s*e*t	*o*t	n*o*:v	d*e*:z
Corsican	sei	sette	ottu	nove	Dece
Umbrian	séi	sétte	òtto	nòe	Dèsce
Neapolitan	sèië	sèttë	òttë	nòvë	Riécë
Sicilian	sie	setti	òttu	novi	dèci
Romanian	s,ase	s,apte	opt	nouâ	zece
Arumanian	s,ase	s,apte	optu	noauâ	**date**
Meglenite	s,asi	s,apti	uopt	nou	ze**t**i
Istriot	s,åse	s,åpte	opt	devet	deset
Sardinian	ses	sette	otto	nove	deghe
Celtic					
Proto-Celtic+	svex	septn	octô	nevn	decn
Gaulish+	suex	sextan	*oxtû	*navan	decam
Brythonic (P-Celtic)					
Welsh	chwech	saith	wyth	naw	deg
Cardiganshire	sich	soch	nîch	noch	dê
Breton	c'hwec'h	seizh	eizh	nav	dek
Vannetais	huéh	seih	eih	naù	dek
Unified Cornish+	whegh	seyth	eath	naw	dek
Common	hwegh	seyth	eth	naw	deg
Modern	whee	sith	eath	nawe	deeg
Devonian+	hueh	seith	eith	nau	dek

Goidelic (Q-Celtic)					
Old Irish+	se	secht	ocht	noi	Deich
Irish	sé	seacht	ocht	naoi	Deich
Scots Gaelic	sia	seachd	ochd	naoi	Deich
Manx	shey	shiaght	hoght	nuy	Jeih
Hellenic					
Mycenean Greek+	we- (*wex-)			e-ne-wo *ennew-	
Classical Greek+	héx	heptá	októ:	ennéa	Déka
Greek	éksi	eftá	oxtó	ennéa	Dhéka
Cypriot	éksi	eftá	oxtó	eniá	Dhéga
Tsakonian	ékse	eftá	oxtó	enía	Dhéka
Tocharian					
Tocharian A+	**s**äk	**s**pät	okät	ñu	s'äk
Tocharian B+	**s**kas	**s**ukt	okt	ñu	s'ak
Albanian					
Albanian	gjashtë	shtatë	tetë	nëntë	Dhjetë
Gheg (Qosaj)	gh'asht	shtat	tet	nân	Dhet
Tosk (Mandritsa)	g'áshtë	shtátë	tétë	në'ntë	Zjétë
Armenian					
+Classical Armenian	vec^{h}	evt^{h}n	ut^{h}	inn	t'asn
Armenian	vec	yot^{h}	ut^{h}	inn	Tas
Baltic					
West					
Old Prussian+	*usjai	*septi:njai	*asto:njai	*newi:njai	desi:mtan
East					
Lithuanian	sheshì	septynì	ashtuonì	devynì	de:shimt

Latvian	seshi	septini	astôni	devini	Desmit
Latgalian	seshi	septeni	ostoni	deveni	Desmit
Slavic					
East					
Russian	shesth shest'	semh sem'	vósemh vósem'	dévÁth dévyat'	désÁth désyat'
Belarussian	shesthh shesc'	sem sem	vósem vósem	dzévÁthh dzéviac'	dzésÁthh dzésiac'
Ukrainian	sh--sth shist'	s--m sim	v°s--m vísim	dév'Áth devyat'	désÁth desyat'
West					
Polish	szes'c'	siedem	osiem	dziewie,c'	dziesie,c'
Kashubian	shesc	sétmë	woesmë	dzevjin'c	dzesin'c
Polabian+	sist	sidêm	visêm	diva,t	disa,t
Czech	shest	sedm	osm	devêt	deset
Slovak	shest'	sedem	osem	devät'	desat'
West	shest	sedem	ossem	devat	desat
East	shesc	shedzem	osem	dzevec	dzeshec
Upper Sorbian	shêsc'	sydom	wosom	dz'ewjec'	dz'esac'
Lower Sorbian	sêsc'	sedym	wosym	z'ewjes'	z'ases'
South					
Old Church Slavonic+	shesti	sedmi	osmi	deve,ti	dese,ti
Bulgarian	shest	sédem	ósem	dévet	Déset
Macedonian	shest	sedum	osum	devet	Deset
Serbo-Croat	shêst	sëdam	ösam	dëve:t	dëse:t
Slovene	shest	sedem	osem	devet	Deset

Anatolian					
Hittite+		shipta-			
Luwian+			*haktau	*nu-	
Lycian+			aitãta	ñuñtãta	
Indo-Iranian					
Proto-Indo-Iranian+	*(k)swacsh	*sapta	*ashta:	*nawa	*daca
Iranian					
Eastern					
Ossetian Iron	æxsæz	avd	ast	farast	Dæs
Digor	æxsæz	avd	ast	farast	Dæs
Avestan+	xshuuash	hapta	ashta	nauua	Dasa
Khwarezmian+	'x	'bhd	'sht	sh'dh	Dhs
Sogdian+	wghwshw	'Bt	'sht	nw'	
Yaghnobi	uxsh	avd	asht	naw	Das
Bactrian+					
Saka+	k**s**äta'	hauda	ha**s**ta	nau	Dasau
Pashto	shpag	ow^{é}	at^{é}	n^{e}	l^{e}s
Wakhi	sha:d	yb	at	na:w	Dhas
Munji	a:xshe	avde	ashkie	nau	Dah
Yidgha	uxsho	avdo	ashcho	nov	Los
Ishkashmi	xu,l	uvd	ot	naw	Da
Sanglechi		haft	ha:**t**		Das
Shughn	xo:gh	wu:vd	waxt	no:w	dhi:s
Rushani	xu:,w	wu:vd	waxt	no:w	Dhes
Yazgulami	xu	uvd	uxt	nu	dhu,s
Sarikoli (Tashkorghani)	xel	üvd	woxt	new	Dhes
Parachi	xi	ho:t	'osht	no:	do:s

Ormuri	sh.^{a}h	ho:	ha:nsht	n^{a}h	Das
Western					
Northwest					
Parthian+	shwh	hft			
Yazdi	shash	haf	hash		
Nayini					De
Natanzi	shæsh	haft	hasht	noh	d'e
Khunsari	shäsh	häft	häsht	no:^{u}	de:^{i}
Gazi	shösh	häf	häsh	nô:^{u}	de:
Sivandi	shush	häf	häsh	nu	da
Vafsi	shish	haf	hash	no	dah
Semnani	shash	haf	hash	na	das
Sangisari	shash	haft	hasht	na	das
Gilaki	shish	haf	hash	noh	da
Mazanderani	shesh	haft	hasht	ne	da
Talysh	shash	håft	hasht	nav	då
Harzani	shosh				doh
Zaza	shesh	**h**ewt	**h**esht	new	des
Gorani	shIsh	hawt	hasht	no	da
Baluchi	sh^{e}sh	h^{e}pt	h^{e}sht	nw	d^{e}h
Turkmenistan	shash	apt	asht	no:	da
E Hill	shash	hapt	hasht	nuh	dah
Rakhshani (Western)	sh^{e}shsh	(h)^{e}pt	(h)^{e}sht	nw	d^{e}
Kermanji (S) Kurdish	shash	hawt	hasht	no:	da
Zaza (N) Kurdish	shash	haft	hasht	na	Da
Bajalani	shish	ha:ft	hasht	nu:	Da
Kermanshahi	shäsh	häft	häsht	nö^	dé:
Southwest					

Old Persian+			*ashta	*nava	*datha
Pahlavi+	shash	haft	hasht	nuh	Dah
Farsi	shesh	haft	hasht	noh	Dah
Isfahani	shish	haf	hash	no:	Da
Tajik	shash	h=aft	h=asht	nu:h=	dah=
Tati	shæsh	hæft	hæsht	ny"h	Dæh
Chali	shesh	haft	hasht	nö	da:
Fars	shisht	häft	häst	nu	das'a
Lari	Shish	'aft	'asht	no	Da
Luri	Shish	haf	hash	nuh	Dah
Kumzari	Shish	haf'ta	hash'ta	na'hata	da'hata
Nuristani					
Ashkun	**sh**û:	su:t	o:**sht**	n**o:**	Dus
Wasi-weri	wu:**sh**	sëtë	a:stë	nu:~	Lezë
Kati	**Sh**u	sut	u**sh**t	nu	Duc
Kalasha-ala	**sh**u:	so:t	o:**sht**	nu:~	do:sh
Indic					
Prakrit+	ch`a	satta	a**tt**a	n.ava	Dasa
Ardhamagadhi+	Cha	satta	a**tt**ha	nava	Dasa
Pali+	Cha	satta	a**tt**ha	nava	Dasa
Romany (Gypsy)					
Spanish	Jol	estér	ostor	nébel	Esden
Welsh	Shov	trin t'a: shto:r	du:vari: shto:r	shto:rt'a: pansh	idesh
Kalderash	Shov	yeftá	oxtó	in'yá	Desh
Syrian	sha:s	h.o:**t**	h.aish**t**	na:	da:s
Armenian	shesh	haft	ha:sht	nu	Dê
Iranian	Shov	efdá:	óxto	enná	Desh
Sinhalese-Maldivian					

Sinhalese	Haya	hata	a**t**a	namaya	Dahaya
Vedda	pahamay tavaekam ay	paham aydeka may	pahamay tunamay	pahamay hatarama y	pahama ytavapa hamay
Maldivian	Haie	hate	ashe	nue	Diha
Northern India					
Dardic					
Kashmiri	shah	sat	$^{e:}$**th**	naw	da
Shina	**sh**a	sât	Â~**sh**	nau~	daï
Brokskat	**s**a	sa:t̲	A:**st**	nu	da:sh
Phalura	**sh**o^{h}	sa:t	A:**sht**	nu:~	da:sh
Bashkarik	sho:	sat	a**th**	num	dash
Tirahi	xo	sat	axt	nab	dah
Torwali	sho:	sat	a**t**	no:m	dash
Wotapuri	sho:	sat	a**t**	nau	dash
Maiya	sho:h	sa:t	a:**th**	nau~	dash
Kalasha	**sh**o	sat	a**sht**	nõ	dash
Khowar	chhoy	sot	osht	nyuf	josh
Dameli	**sh**o	sat	a**sh**t	nõ:	dash
Gawar-bati	**sh**^{u}o:	s^{e}t	o:**st**	nu:~	dosh
Pashai	**ch**ha	sa:ta	a:**sht**a	na:w	da:y
Shumashti	**sho**o	sa	â**sh**t	nu:	däs
Nangalami	**s**o:	sat	õ:**st**	nu:~	das
Dumaki	**sh**a	sot	o**sh**t	nau	dai
Western					
Marathi	s^{e}ha	sat	a**t**h	n^{e}u	d^{e}ha
Konkani	sô	sat	atth	nov	dha
Sindhi	cha	sata	atha	nava	**dd**aha
Khatri	cho	sat	ath	nu	Dô
Lahnda	ch`e:	satt	a**tt**`	nå~	**d**a:h

Central					
Hindi/ Urdu	c^hai	sa:t	a:**t**h	nau	Das
Parya	ch^he	sat	a**t**	nu	Das
Punjabi	che	s^et	^{e}**t**	n^ewng	d^es
Siraiki	chi	sat	a**t**h	naõ	Dah
Gujarati	ch^e	sat	a**t**h	n^ev	d^es
Rajasthani (Marwari)	ch\`aw	sa:t	a:**t**\`	naw	Das
Banjari (Lamani)	Cho	saat	aaT	naw	Das
Malvi	ch\`e:	sa:t	a:**t**\`	naw	Das
Bhili	so:	xa:t	a:**t**\`	naw	Dax
Dogri	ch\`e:	sat	a**t**\`	nau	Das
Kumauni	ch\`ai	sa:t	a:**t**\`	nau	Das
Garhwali	ch\`ai:	sa:t	a:**t**\`	nau	Das
W Pahari	tsho:	sa:**t**	a:**t**:h	no:	do:sh
Khandeshi	ch\`a	sa:t	a:**t**\`	naü	Das
East Central					
Nepali	Cha	sa:t	a:**t**	nau	Das
Maithili	ch\`a:	sa:t	a:**t**'	náu	Dash
Magahi	Chau	sat	a:**t**h	nau	Das
Bhojpuri	c^hæ	sa:t	a:$\mathbf{t}^h$	nao	Das
Awadhi (Kosali)	cha:	sa:t	a:**t**h	nuu	Dus
Chattisgarhi	ch\`e:	sa:t	a:**t**\`	no:	Das
Eastern					
Oriya	cha'a	saat	aa**t**h	na'a	Dash
Bengali	choy	sat	a**t**	noy	Dosh
Assamese	s^ei	xat	a**t**h	n^e	d^eh
Mayang	soy	ha:d	a:t	nau	Dos
Elamite					

Elamite+					
Northwest					
Brahui	shash	haft	hasht	no:	Dah
Northeast					
Kurukh	soyye:	satte:	a**tt**he:	nai**m**ye:	dasse:
Malto	so:ye	sa:te	a:**t**e	noye	da:se
Central					
Kolami	saa / a:r	sa.t	a.t	nov	daa
Naiki					
Parji	se:je:n				
Gadaba	a:ru-gur				padi-mandi
Telugu	aaru	eedu	enimidi	tommidi	padi
Gondi	sa:ru:ng	e:**r**u:ng	armur	anma	putth
Koya	a:ru	e:**d**u	ennimidi	tommidi	padi
Konda	a:ru	e:**r**u			
Manda					
Pengo	co	sa**t**	at	nov	das
Kui	sajgi	odgi	a:**t**u	na	dashu
Kuvi	so:	sa:ta	a:**t**a	no:	dos
South					
Tulu	a:ji	**e:**l	e**n**ma	ormba	patt
Koraga	aji	eli			pattu
Kannada	aaru	eeLu	eNTu	ombattu	Hattu
Badaga	a:ru	iyyu	e**tt**u	ombattu	Attu
Kodagu	a:r^{ü}	ye:**l**^{ü}	ye**tt**^{ü}	oyimbad ü	patt^{ü}
Kurumba	-a.rʉ̱	-ö.**l**ʉ̱	-ö**tt**ʉ̱	-embadʉ̱	-pattʉ̱
Toda	o:**r**	öw	ö**t**	Wïnboth	Pot
Kota	a:re	ye:ye	ye**tt**e	vorapa:d	Patte

				e	
Tamil	aarru	aezhu	a:ddu	Onpathu	paththu
Malayalam	a:ru	e:lu	ettu	Onpatu	Pattu
Irula	aru	elu	yettu	vombadu	Pattu
Nahali					
Nahali	cha:h	sato	atho	Nav	Das
Burushashki					
Hunza	mishíndi	thalé	altámbi	Huntí	Tóorim i
Yasin	bishínde	thalé	altámbe	Hutí	Tórom
Basque					
Ancient Basque+				bade-eratsi	
Basque	sei	Zazpi	zortzi	bederatzi	Hamar
Etruscan					
Etruscan	sa	semph	Cezp	enva?	Zar
Hurrian					
Hurrian	--	shindia	--	Nizhi	Eman

References

1. *Āpastamba Śrauta Sūtra* (*Āśs.*), 1953 : ed. Vidwan T. Shriniwas Gopalacharya, Mysore.

2. (i) (Dr.) Arya, Ravi Prakash, 2007: *Vedic and Classical Sanskrit.* Indian Foundation for Vedic Science, Delhi.

(ii) (Dr.) Arya, Ravi Prakash, 1991: *Researches into Vedic and Linguistic Studies*, Grantha Bharati Prakashan, Delhi.

3. (Dr.) Bhārtiya, Bhawanilal Vs. 2042: *PūnāPravacana,* Vedic Pustakalaya, Ajmer.

4. (Dr.) Gopal, Ram 1983: *History and Principles of Vedic interpretations.* Concept Publishing company. Delhi.

5. (It. Col.) Kennedy. Vans 1828: *Researches into the Origin and Affinity of the Principal languages of Asia and Europe.* London.

6. Monier Williams, M.: *A Sanskrit English Dictionary*, Motilal Banarssidas, Delhi, 2002.

7. Macdonell, A. A.: *A Vedic Grammar*, Strassburg, 1910.

8. *Nirukta* (*Nir.*) :Nirukta of Yāska, Ed. Rajawade, V.K. Poona, BORI, 1940.

9. Pāṇini (Pāṇ.): *Aṣṭādhyāyī.* Chowkhamba Sanskrit series office, Varanasi. 1950.

10. *Ṛgveda* (*RV.*): Ed. & Tr. in Sanskrit and Hindi by Swami Dayanand, Ajmer.

11. *Satyārtha Prakash* (S.P.): By Swami Dayanand. Saraswati. Ramlal Kapoor Trust, Bahalgarh, Haryana, 1974.

12. Serjeantson, Mary S. 1935: *A History of Foreign Words in English*, London.

13. *Vārttika (Vār.):* Kāryāyana's *vārttikas*on Pāṇinian*Sūtras.* See Mabābhāṣya ed. Vedavrata, Rohtak, Haryana. 1963.

14. Wackerganel, J.: *Altindische Grammatik*, Göttingen,

Vandenhock& Ruprecht, 1954.

15. Whitney W.D.: *Sanskrit Grammar*, Harward, 1955.

www.ingramcontent.com/pod-product-compliance
Lightning Source LLC
Chambersburg PA
CBHW071308040426
42444CB00009B/1919
* 9 7 8 8 1 8 7 7 1 0 2 7 1 *